An history of angells being a theologicall treatise of our communion and warre with them: handled on the 6th chapter of the Ephesians, the 11, 12, 13, 14, 15, 16, 17, 18 verses / by Henry Lawrence ... (1649)

John Milton

Early English Books Online (EEBO) Editions

Imagine holding history in your hands.

Now you can. Digitally preserved and previously accessible only through libraries as Early English Books Online, this rare material is now available in single print editions. Thousands of books written between 1475 and 1700 and ranging from religion to astronomy, medicine to music, can be delivered to your doorstep in individual volumes of high-quality historical reproductions.

We have been compiling these historic treasures for more than 70 years. Long before such a thing as "digital" even existed, ProQuest founder Eugene Power began the noble task of preserving the British Museum's collection on microfilm. He then sought out other rare and endangered titles, providing unparalleled access to these works and collaborating with the world's top academic institutions to make them widely available for the first time. This project furthers that original vision.

These texts have now made the full journey -- from their original printing-press versions available only in rare-book rooms to online library access to new single volumes made possible by the partnership between artifact preservation and modern printing technology. A portion of the proceeds from every book sold supports the libraries and institutions that made this collection possible, and that still work to preserve these invaluable treasures passed down through time.

This is history, traveling through time since the dawn of printing to your own personal library.

Initial Proquest EEBO Print Editions collections include:

Early Literature

This comprehensive collection begins with the famous Elizabethan Era that saw such literary giants as Chaucer, Shakespeare and Marlowe, as well as the introduction of the sonnet. Traveling through Jacobean and Restoration literature, the highlight of this series is the Pollard and Redgrave 1475-1640 selection of the rarest works from the English Renaissance.

Early Documents of World History

This collection combines early English perspectives on world history with documentation of Parliament records, royal decrees and military documents that reveal the delicate balance of Church and State in early English government. For social historians, almanacs and calendars offer insight into daily life of common citizens. This exhaustively complete series presents a thorough picture of history through the English Civil War.

Historical Almanacs

Historically, almanacs served a variety of purposes from the more practical, such as planting and harvesting crops and plotting nautical routes, to predicting the future through the movements of the stars. This collection provides a wide range of consecutive years of "almanacks" and calendars that depict a vast array of everyday life as it was several hundred years ago.

Early History of Astronomy & Space

Humankind has studied the skies for centuries, seeking to find our place in the universe. Some of the most important discoveries in the field of astronomy were made in these texts recorded by ancient stargazers, but almost as impactful were the perspectives of those who considered their discoveries to be heresy. Any independent astronomer will find this an invaluable collection of titles arguing the truth of the cosmic system.

Early History of Industry & Science

Acting as a kind of historical Wall Street, this collection of industry manuals and records explores the thriving industries of construction; textile, especially wool and linen; salt; livestock; and many more.

Early English Wit, Poetry & Satire

The power of literary device was never more in its prime than during this period of history, where a wide array of political and religious satire mocked the status quo and poetry called humankind to transcend the rigors of daily life through love, God or principle. This series comments on historical patterns of the human condition that are still visible today.

Early English Drama & Theatre

This collection needs no introduction, combining the works of some of the greatest canonical writers of all time, including many plays composed for royalty such as Queen Elizabeth I and King Edward VI. In addition, this series includes history and criticism of drama, as well as examinations of technique.

Early History of Travel & Geography

Offering a fascinating view into the perception of the world during the sixteenth and seventeenth centuries, this collection includes accounts of Columbus's discovery of the Americas and encompasses most of the Age of Discovery, during which Europeans and their descendants intensively explored and mapped the world. This series is a wealth of information from some the most groundbreaking explorers.

Early Fables & Fairy Tales

This series includes many translations, some illustrated, of some of the most well-known mythologies of today, including Aesop's Fables and English fairy tales, as well as many Greek, Latin and even Oriental parables and criticism and interpretation on the subject.

Early Documents of Language & Linguistics

The evolution of English and foreign languages is documented in these original texts studying and recording early philology from the study of a variety of languages including Greek, Latin and Chinese, as well as multilingual volumes, to current slang and obscure words. Translations from Latin, Hebrew and Aramaic, grammar treatises and even dictionaries and guides to translation make this collection rich in cultures from around the world.

Early History of the Law

With extensive collections of land tenure and business law "forms" in Great Britain, this is a comprehensive resource for all kinds of early English legal precedents from feudal to constitutional law, Jewish and Jesuit law, laws about public finance to food supply and forestry, and even "immoral conditions." An abundance of law dictionaries, philosophy and history and criticism completes this series.

Early History of Kings, Queens and Royalty

This collection includes debates on the divine right of kings, royal statutes and proclamations, and political ballads and songs as related to a number of English kings and queens, with notable concentrations on foreign rulers King Louis IX and King Louis XIV of France, and King Philip II of Spain. Writings on ancient rulers and royal tradition focus on Scottish and Roman kings, Cleopatra and the Biblical kings Nebuchadnezzar and Solomon.

Early History of Love, Marriage & Sex

Human relationships intrigued and baffled thinkers and writers well before the postmodern age of psychology and self-help. Now readers can access the insights and intricacies of Anglo-Saxon interactions in sex and love, marriage and politics, and the truth that lies somewhere in between action and thought.

Early History of Medicine, Health & Disease

This series includes fascinating studies on the human brain from as early as the 16th century, as well as early studies on the physiological effects of tobacco use. Anatomy texts, medical treatises and wound treatment are also discussed, revealing the exponential development of medical theory and practice over more than two hundred years.

Early History of Logic, Science and Math

The "hard sciences" developed exponentially during the 16th and 17th centuries, both relying upon centuries of tradition and adding to the foundation of modern application, as is evidenced by this extensive collection. This is a rich collection of practical mathematics as applied to business, carpentry and geography as well as explorations of mathematical instruments and arithmetic; logic and logicians such as Aristotle and Socrates; and a number of scientific disciplines from natural history to physics.

Early History of Military, War and Weaponry

Any professional or amateur student of war will thrill at the untold riches in this collection of war theory and practice in the early Western World. The Age of Discovery and Enlightenment was also a time of great political and religious unrest, revealed in accounts of conflicts such as the Wars of the Roses.

Early History of Food

This collection combines the commercial aspects of food handling, preservation and supply to the more specific aspects of canning and preserving, meat carving, brewing beer and even candy-making with fruits and flowers, with a large resource of cookery and recipe books. Not to be forgotten is a "the great eater of Kent," a study in food habits.

Early History of Religion

From the beginning of recorded history we have looked to the heavens for inspiration and guidance. In these early religious documents, sermons, and pamphlets, we see the spiritual impact on the lives of both royalty and the commoner. We also get insights into a clergy that was growing ever more powerful as a political force. This is one of the world's largest collections of religious works of this type, revealing much about our interpretation of the modern church and spirituality.

Early Social Customs

Social customs, human interaction and leisure are the driving force of any culture. These unique and quirky works give us a glimpse of interesting aspects of day-to-day life as it existed in an earlier time. With books on games, sports, traditions, festivals, and hobbies it is one of the most fascinating collections in the series.

The BiblioLife Network

This project was made possible in part by the BiblioLife Network (BLN), a project aimed at addressing some of the huge challenges facing book preservationists around the world. The BLN includes libraries, library networks, archives, subject matter experts, online communities and library service providers. We believe every book ever published should be available as a high-quality print reproduction; printed on-demand anywhere in the world. This insures the ongoing accessibility of the content and helps generate sustainable revenue for the libraries and organizations that work to preserve these important materials.

The following book is in the "public domain" and represents an authentic reproduction of the text as printed by the original publisher. While we have attempted to accurately maintain the integrity of the original work, there are sometimes problems with the original work or the micro-film from which the books were digitized. This can result in minor errors in reproduction. Possible imperfections include missing and blurred pages, poor pictures, markings and other reproduction issues beyond our control. Because this work is culturally important, we have made it available as part of our commitment to protecting, preserving, and promoting the world's literature.

GUIDE TO FOLD-OUTS MAPS and OVERSIZED IMAGES

The book you are reading was digitized from microfilm captured over the past thirty to forty years. Years after the creation of the original microfilm, the book was converted to digital files and made available in an online database.

In an online database, page images do not need to conform to the size restrictions found in a printed book. When converting these images back into a printed bound book, the page sizes are standardized in ways that maintain the detail of the original. For large images, such as fold-out maps, the original page image is split into two or more pages

Guidelines used to determine how to split the page image follows:

• Some images are split vertically; large images require vertical and horizontal splits.
• For horizontal splits, the content is split left to right.
• For vertical splits, the content is split from top to bottom.
• For both vertical and horizontal splits, the image is processed from top left to bottom right.

AN
History of Angells,

BEING A
Theologicall TREATISE of our
Communion and Warre with them.

Handled on the 6th Chapter of the *Ephesians*,
the 11, 12, 13, 14, 15, 16, 17, 18. Verses.

By HENRY LAWRENCE, a Member
of this present PARLIAMENT.

LONDON;
Printed by *M.S.* and are to be sold by *William
Nealand* in *Duck Lane*, 1 6 4 9.

To my

Moſt deare and Moſt ho-
nour'd Mother,

THE LADY

LAWRENCE.

Moſt honour'd Mother,

Vring this buſy time,
in the which our coun-
try (ſubjected to thoſe calamities, of which by faith
we ſee the cataſtrophe
glorious) hath becne the
ſtage of ſo much action, and the field
of ſo many battailles, my lot was caſt to be

*   from

from home, and in this retirement, if I injoyed not the happinesse of his wish, to have *otium cum dignitate*, leisure with dignity, (for I pretend but to an excuse) yet it was without any just cause of reproach, for the warre found me abroad, not sent me thither, and I have beene onely wary without a just and warrantable reason, to ingage my selfe in that condition, from which a providence seem'd to rescue mee. But of all the peeces of our life, wee are accountable for those of our greatest leisure, whereas publike and visible imployment gives its owne account. It was said of *Cato, that hee conflicted with manners, as Scipio did with enemyes*; The conflict with manners, as it is a kind of warre, from which no condition will free us, so leisure and retirement is commonly the opportunity of it; for such enemyes will find us soonest in that condition, as on the other side, wee have an advantage by it, to seeke out, and improove all the strengthes, and aides, that are requisite for our owne defence, and the incommodating of our enemyes. In this warre therefore, to which my leisure more eminently expos'd pos'd me, and to which also it more fitted & determin'd me, I was diversly acted, according to the severall methods, and occasions of warre, by the great Generall of all his people *Iesus Christ*, sometimes conflicting with the knowne, otherwhiles persuing the discoveryes of the unknowne corruptions of my owne heart, and others. I found assuredly, *That a mans foes vvere them of his ovvne houshold, and that to be delivered from the ill men our selves, vvas to be avovved as a rich and high mercy.* But as most warres, that have their rise and beginnings at home, and from within, are not determin'd, and concluded within that circle, but to greaten and assure their party, and prevailing, seeke the assistance of forreigne aides, or find (at least) their homebred differences and divisions made use of by neighbouring powers, who while they pretend to helpe their friends, serve themselves, or some third state, to which their proper interests ingages and determines them: So did I conceave, that in this spirituall warre, there were not wanting aides and assistances from without, that were of mighty influence in the businesse of our fight-

* 2   ing,

ing, and who by ſtratagems, and methods, as well as by fine force, contributed exceedingly, not onely to the laſt iſſue of the warre, but to the ſucceſſe almoſt of every battaille. And theſe, though they were of wonderfull moment, yet me thought were generally little conſidered, but men terminated their thoughts within the compaſſe of themſelves, or if they went farther, lookt preſently, and immediately upon God, (as in every thing it is an eaſy and vulgar ſtep from the laſt effect to the higheſt cauſe) whereas thoſe hoaſts of Angells, which on either ſide more immediatly managed and improoved this warre, as they are ſpirituall and inviſible beings, ſo they paſſe with us, unſeene, and undiſcerned, in a great proportion; and we, who are the ſubjects of this warre, and whoſe intereſts are eſpecially concern'd in it, by not knowing or conſidering, can neither improve our moſt active, and moſt powerfull friends, or enemyes, to our advantage. I was guided therefore by ſuch thoughts as theſe to the enſuing meditations: and as we uſually are more ſenſible of our enemyes then our friends, ſo the

firſt

first defigne I had , was to difcover what influence the evill Angells have upon us, and our actions,what parts they act,& how they communicate themfelves to us,and affect us for ill. But as commonly things have not the fame place in the execution, which they have in the defigne, fo I found it neceffary in the method of this difcourfe, to confider firft of the Angells in their pure naturalls, and then, (as of the moft eminent patterne of Angelicall power and influence) of the good Angells, and after that, (with the due difference of the abate of power and ftrength which finne had cauf'd) of the influence,and effects,which the evill Angells have upon mankind , which every one experienceth,though few, enough know it or confider it.

And becaufe in a fubject of this nature, nothing is more eafy , then to wander even to the loofing of our felves in the fpeculative part , I endevoured to remedy that inconvenience throughout , by certaine practicall Corollaryes , which might reduce the notionall part of the difcourfe to the ufe and end intended , and might let us

fee

see how much our interest is concern'd in the right knowing and improoving these mighty spirits. And lastly, because the Scripture I first pitcht my thoughts upon in order to these things, furnisht me with proper armes for this holy warre, I judg'd it would be a good accesse to this discourse (of which also it might constitute a third part) to shew those armes, and to give what light I could to the right wearing and using of them.

For other thinges I, pretend neither to such a method, or language, or what ever else of that kinde, as is wont to begett a reputation with many readers; for besides the vanity of such affectations in a subject especially so serious, these thoughts were form'd for a more private use, then their present condition leads them to; nay such thinges as were but necessary, as a division of this discourse into chapters (of which it was easily capable) a more correct printing, and some other perfectings of a like consideration, have by reason of the busines of my owne occasion, and a mistake somewhere, beene wanting; this
I pre-

I pretend to, to magnifie God in those mighty hoasts of spirituall substances, which he manageth wonderfully and differently, for the good of his children; to gratifie and serve the good Angels, who (if I may judge of others by my self) have been too little considered, in order to them, or our selves; and to professe, and (as much as in me lyes) to assist, to an irreconcileable, and everlasting warre, with the greatest and most inveterate enemies of God and man, the divell and his Angells: And last of all (which I mention'd in the beginning) to give one instance, that I have not beene idle in these busy times, nor without the thoughts, and designes of warre, in an age, when warre is become almost the profession of all men. Why I inscribe these papers to you, *My dearest Mother*, will neede no larger account then this; *Nature and your ovvne goodnesse, have form'd you ablest, to pardon me in any thing, vvherein I shall neede it; And of all I have knovvne of either Sexe, I have mett vvith fevv more diligently inquisitive, or pertinently reasoning of things of a raised and abstracted nature, (especially vvhich might have influence into the good of another life)*

then

then your self. To which I adde, *That I pro-*
fesse to have infinite ingagements, to avovv my self
before all the vvorld

Most honoured Mother

Your most obedient Sonne

&

Most Humble servant

HENRY LAWRENCE.

A Treatise of our Communion and warre with Angells.

Ephes. 6. 11. 12. 13. 14. 15. 16. 17. 18.

Put on the whole Armour of God, that ye may be able to stand against the wiles of the Divell; For wee wrestle not against flesh and blood, but against principalities, against powers, against the Rulers of the Darknes of this world, against spirituall wickednesse in high places, &c.

HE great externall cause of all our evills is the Divell, who hath such a kinde of relation to our sins, as the holy Spirit hath to our graces, saving that hee findes a foundation within us to build upon, matter out of which hee extracts his formes, whereas the holy Spirit doth that worke as well as the other, and is put to the paine of foundation worke as well as building. I call him the externall cause in opposition to the working of our owne corruptions, which are our owne properly, and most of all within us. In other respects hee may be sayd to be the internall cause also, for hee mingles himselfe with our most intimate corruptions, and the Seate of his warfare is the inward man. Now because hee hath a greater influence into us then perhaps wee consider of, and the knowledge of our enemy is of great concernement to the warre wee must have with him, I desire a litle to inquire into this mighty enemy of God and man, that wee may knowe him, and dread him,

A

him, fo farre as to fit us for conflict, and that wee may knowe him and difcover him, for hee is a perfect Iugler, hee raignes not much when his tricks are difcovered, and that wee may knowe him and refift him, if hee fhall embolden himfelfe to ftand his ground as often hee doth.

The Apoftle from the beginning of the 4 Chap. had taught them how they fhould live in generall, firft among themfelves, then with relation to thofe that are without, ver. 18. Then hee condifcends to particuler duties of Hufbands and Wives, Parents and Children, Mafters and Servants, and laft of all before hee concludes, returnes to that which hee had mentioned in the 3. Chap. ver. 16. where hee beggs of God as the moft defireable thing in the world, *that they might be ftrengthened according to the riches of his grace in the inner man*: Heere hee turnes his prayer into an exhortation, wherein hee provokes them *to be ftrong in the Lord, and in the power of his might*, ver. 10. That is to fay, though you have all faith and all knowledge, and worke well, yet you muft perfevere, yee muft goe on, and you muft doe it with ftrength: It is a great matter to come into the lifts, but it is great to runne alfo, and to fight when you are there, for you fhall meete with thofe that fhall oppofe you and conflict with you, therefore *be ftrong in the Lord, and in the power of his might*, that is with the Lord by his Spirit, which is his mighty Agent fhall worke in your hearts; Be not ftrong in your owne ftrength, in your owne purpofes, in the freedome of your owne wills, fo was *Peter*, who got nothing by it, but in the Lord, his Spirit can ftrengthen, can raife, can confirme you.

Ver. 11. *Put you on the whole Armour of God*; God is able to preferve you, but hee will doe it by your fighting,
                                                                and

and your Armour muſt be ſutable to the hand that
wields it , which is the Spirit of God in you , and the
enemy it conflicts with, which is the Divell : Againe,
it muſt be *the whole Armour* , if you want any one piece,
that place will be expoſed to danger , alſo , *All* , for offence, and defence , that you may ſave your ſelf by deſtroying your enemy , *that yee may bee able to ſtand againſt*
the wiles of the Divell, that is , that yee may hold your
ground though you ſhould receive wounds, and thruſts
yet that you may not give way, as ver. 13. *that yee*
may withſtand in the evill day ; The day of temptation
is an evill day , a day of trouble , a day of tryall , and
often in reſpect of the event , *evill* , therefore *deliver us*
from evill : And having done all to ſtand , that is , if you
doe all in this fight God commaunds you, and omit nothing , by the vertue of God, you will ſtand, but there
is no dallying with ſuch an enemy , your ſtanding muſt
be a fruit and reſult of doing all.

  The wiles of the Divell; the word is *Methods*, that is, the
divell like a cunning fencer hath his faints, knowes how
to take his advantages , and like a great commaunder
hath his ſtratagemes , by which hee doth as much as by
fine force , and theſe are well laid , there is a Method in
them to make the worke the ſurer , one thing depends
upon another , and all contribute to make the reſult
firme.

  For wee wraſtle, that is, *de conflictu, eſt ſermo, non de ludo,*
we ſpeake of conflicts, not of play, or ſport ; *not againſt*
Fleſh and Blood, that is , that which wee have onely in
our eye is fleſh and blood , wicked men that wounds us
and perſecute us, where note, that God calls all wicked
men , all the enemies of his Church, but *fleſh and blood*;
now they are the moſt periſhable things when God
will blowe upon them , *for all fleſh is graſſe* ; though the

A 2   enemies

enemies be never so great and mighty, they are but as grasse and stubble.

Or secondly *flesh and blood*, by which may be understood your carnall lusts, the concupiscence of the flesh, and the boyling and ebullition of the blood to anger, and all passions, it is not so much, or it is not especially against these you wrestle, but rather against him that acts them, and makes use of them to your ruine and dis-advantage, which is the divell, and this hee may perhaps speake against the opinion of the Heathen, who understood not the operation of the divell, but thought all our conflicts was against internall passions.

But against Principalities, hee seemes to describe the divels heere which are our enemies, first from the principality of their nature, by which the eminency and raisednes of their nature in respect of this visible world is set forth, that as the state of Princes differ eminently from other men, so the nature of divells, as Princes, excells the nature of men and of all visible things.

Against Powers; hee calls them *Powers* simply without any addition to shewe the eminency of their power, aswell as of their natures, that as they have a nature, farre above flesh and blood, fitted for great things, so they have a power sutable and fitted to act this nature, as may be seene by their effects, both upon us and upon the world, though wee are not so to judge of their power as the *Manichees*, who feigned two supreame powers a good and a bad; which conflicted perpetually each with other, for their power falls as farre below Gods, as it is above us, and infinitely more.

Against the Rulers of the darknesse of this world: Heere the Divels are described from the universall dominion they have in this world; they are called *the Rulers of the darknesse of this world*, to shewe what the Divell is conversant about,

about, all his worke is to bring in darknes, and to shewe principally the seate of his Empire : Hee is not the ruler of the world, that is *Gods Territory*, but of the darknes of this world, the children of darknes ; though hee ceaseth not to interpose, and excercise rule, even over the children of light, and within the Saints, so farre as darknes possesseth them. It is also called *the darknesse of this world*, to shewe the terme of his Empire; it is but in this life, in another himselfe shalbe subject to darknes, and eternall torments.

Against spirituall wickednesse in high places : *Beza* translates it spirituall malices, the words are πνευματικα τ πονερίας, the spirituallnes of evill and wickednesse, carnall wickednesses are inferiour to spirituall wickednesses, which occupieth the highest part of the soule, which possesses the understanding more, and are not laid out in carnall passions, and concupiscences, so as the Divell hath a most excelling malice. Hee layes out himselfe in the excercise of, and provoking us to the most spirituall wickednesses, though hee is in the other also, and labours to make even carnall sins as much spirituall as is possible, by causing them to be acted against light, and against love and engagements.

In high places ; the word is τοις επουρανίοις : *Beza* translates it, *in sublimi*, on high, that is, in high places ; your enemy hath the advantage ground, hee is on high, hee hath gained the hill, hee is in the aire, how mighty an advantage this is in a combate you knowe, but it signifies in *Heavenly*, as in the margent of your bookes, which may have relation aswell to things as places, and then it shewes the things about which his malicious studyes are conversant, that is to take all heavenly things from us, and to deprive us of what ever is heavenly. And now what say you to your Antagonist, heere is a dread-

A 3

full

full enemy formed already, you have heard fables of Giants, heere is a Gyant indeed, great in subtilty, excellent in nature, mighty in power, large in dominion, above all, eminent in ill and malice; wee are apt to feare onely, what wee see, but invisible things are the best and worst, they are the greatest, as our originall sin which wee see not but by its effects; and this great invisible prince that casts so many darts at us, the blowes of which wee feele, but consider not the hand that gives them, whence comes all our mischeife: I would set out this enemy a litle in his owne coulours, that wee may knowe him, and knowe how to deale with him, wee shall surely finde him as blacke as wee can paint him, the ignorance of our evills may cover them, but not relieve them; let us knowe him, and wee shall knowe how to deale with him, there is strength and might in Iesus Christ, God hath but raised him up as Pharoah to make his power knowne upon him, wee have weapons can reach him, and an arme strong enough, but wee must arme our selves, but wee must use it, wee shall overcome, but wee must fight. Put on therefore a firme courage, for before all be done your enemy will appeare extreamely blacke, and dreadfull, and yet to comfort you, *greater is hee that is in you, then hee that is in the world.*

Now for a more perfect knowledge of this great enemy, wee will launch a litle into that comon place, of the nature of Angells, yet keeping neere the Scripture and not departing from our assured rule, the word of God, nor intending so large a compasse of discourse as the thing will beare, though the knowledge of it is of very great use in many respects, but so farre forth as it may afford a full light, to the discourse wee have undertaken.

1.   And first, how excellent soever their nature is, that they are creatures, there is no question, though
Aristotle

Ariftotle will needs have them eternall fubftances, a thing altogether derogatory to God, who onely is eternall, and therefore as the firft caufe, muft needs be the former and maker of all other things: It is true that Mofes doth not particularly defcribe their creation, accommodating himfelfe to the rudeneffe, and ignorance of that time, in which hee writ, and therefore particularizes onely in vifible things.

But that they were created wee have cleare fcripture for it, Coloff. 1. 16. *For by him were all things created, whether in heaven or earth, vifible or invifible, whether they be Thrones or Dominions, or Principalities, or powers, all things were created by him and for him:* Wee fhall not infift heere upon the particuler titles, but you fee heere creation of things in heaven, afwell as in earth, and invifible, afwell as vifible, fo Pfal. 148. 5. *Let them praife the name of the Lord, for hee commanded and they were created.* What was created? all that hee had named before, *the heavens and the Angells.* Hee begins with the firft and moft eminent peeces of creation: If you afke when they were created? certainely not before the created matter of the vifible world, for Mofes faith, *In the beginning God created the heavens and the earth*; if they had bene therefore created before, there fhould have bene a beginning of time, and working before that; befides its faid God wrought all his workes in fixe dayes, and refted the feaventh. If you afke what day they were created? in all likelyhood, the firft day with the fupreame heaven, in refpect of the fimilitude of their nature; they give alfo another reafon Job. 38. 7. *When the morning ftarres fang together, and all the fons of God fhouted for joye,* becaufe they feeme there to applaud God in the workes of his creation: vizt, when the higheft heavens and firft matter was created, out of which other things was formed.   2. Thefe

2.   2. These excellent creatures are true substances, and doe really exist, contrary to the opinion of the *Saduces*, that denied *Angells* and *Spirits*, that is, that thought by the name of Angells was meant nothing but good or ill inspirations, or motions, or els the wonders and apparitions which were wrought by God; but nothing is more absurd then this for.

1.   First they were created, therefore they were substances and not accidents in another subject.

2.   2. They are endowed with understanding and will, by virtue of which they were capable of sinning, and departing from the truth, of obeying, or standing out against God.

3.   3. From their office they appeare before God, they serve God, wee are commaunded to make them our Patternes, they come to us, admonish us of Gods will, they teach, protect and comfort us.

4.   4. From their apparitions and services, they appeared often to the Fathers, they wrastled with Iacob, eate with Abraham, carry the elect into Abrahams bosome, they gather the dead at the day of judgement, and wee shalbe like the Angells; also Christ was said not to take upon him the nature of Angells, and Paul chargeth Timothy before Christ and the elect Angells, and Christ is said to have a name given him above the Angells: Lastly to give a ground out of Philosophy, Aristotle saith that to the perfection of the world it is necessary that there should be three sorts of substances, invisible, visible, and partly invisible and partly visible, as if hee had hit (as indeed hee did) on Gods creation: The second are the heavens and elements, and compositions out of them, the last are Men, which have an invisible soule, and a visible body, and hold the middle, the first therefore must be the
Angells:

Angells : If you aske as an appendix to this, whether
the Angells have bodies, or are altogether incorporall,
it is a question controverted betweene the Philosophers, the Schoolmen, and the Fathers; the Plato-
niste would have them have bodies, to which many of
the Fathers adhere; Aristotle and the Schoolmen
would have them altogether incorporall, the reasons
on both sides are not unworthy considering, if one
would amuse themselves in that, out of which the
Scripture gives no issue, I will not trouble you with it,
onely this, its safe to say, that they are not essences so
simple as they are altogether uncapable of composition, it is onely proper to God to have his being and
essence or substance the same; Angells are mutable,
they consist of an act which they are, and of a power
into which they may be reduced, it is one thing in
them to be simply, and another thing to be indued
with understanding and will, to be and to be good, to
be and to be wise, God onely is *I am*, uncapable of any
change, as of any composition; To say God were an
Angell, were a derogation, as to say hee were a body,
unlesse you should meane by a body, a *substance*, as Ter-
tullian did, and so called God a body, that is, a *substance* :
But if they have any such composition, as may be called a body, it is certainely of the greatest finenesse and
subtilty a spirituall body, and therefore not like to
be of that grossenes that either the aire is, or those
heavens that are framed out of the Chaos, but neerer
the substance of the highest heavens, which seeme to
have bene made at the same time : To conclude, it
will be safe to say that in comparison of God they are
bodies, in comparison of us they are pure and mighty
Spirits. From this that hath bene said in generall, of
the nature of Angells, consider by way of corrollary.

B   First

1.   Firſt in that theſe bleſſed ſubſtances are creatures brought with you by God, out of the ſame wombe of nothing, and raiſed from that loweneſſe to the height and dignity they poſſeſſe, how great then is that God that can make and forme ſuch beings from nothing. Wee praiſe workemen that with all accommodations of inſtruments and matter can produce ſomething worth the looking on, but nothing and ſomething are all alike to God; Alſo hee can make of one lumpe a veſſell of honour, as eaſly as of diſhonour, if the workman be to be eſteemed by the worke; conſider theſe mighty pieces, and who made them, breake into an admiration and bleſſing of God, as David did Pſal. 104. 1. *Bleſſe the Lord, O my ſoule, O Lord my God thou art very great, cloathed with honour and Majeſty,* why hee was able to forme and create thoſe mighty things and among them the Angells, ver. 4. *Who maketh his Angells ſpirits, his Miniſters a flame of fire,* where (by the way) hee gives you their nature and office, for their nature they are ſpirits raiſed and excellent, for that office, they are miniſters.

2.   2. But ſecondly if God created them, then feare them not hee hath a hand over them ſtill, hee that bounds the ſea, will bound the divells, *They are reſerved in chaines,* as well to their effects, as to their *puniſhments,* they cannot breake looſe nor get beyond their Tedder: On the other ſide there are good ones amongſt them, which ſhalbe ordered to your advantage by this maker and creator of them, who mindes us as well as them, and mindes them for us, of which wee have a good pledge in Ieſus Chriſt, *Who tooke not on him the nature of Angells, but tooke on him the ſeed of Abraham,* our *nature* and ſurely all creatures ſhall ſubſerve to that compoſition of which God is a part.

3. If God created the Angells, feare no lowereſſe, God can raiſe you high enough in a minute, can you imagine almoſt greater termes of diſtance, then from nothing to an Angell, wee ſuffer many graduall changes in our bodies and ſoules, but God can raiſe us in a moment, if hee pleaſe, to the higheſt pitches of grace, or comfort, and proſperity.

4. How great is that love to piece up with much care, and paines ſuch veſſells as wee are, who could in a moment caſt new ones of a better forme, and fill his houſe with Angells; but hee loves our tribe, and hath condiſcended to us, and done more for us then for the Angells.

5. You ſee reaſon to conſider of the Angells not as inſpirations, motions, fanſyes, or phantaſmes, but as of reall ſubſtances, and exiſtences, mightie ſpirits, that in the frame of the world and order of nature come neereſt God, and poſſeſſe the next place to him, for ſo they are, and as ſuch are the immediate inſtruments of God, which have ever had much to doe with the ſonnes of men, though ſometimes in apparitions more ſutable to our nature, ſometimes in a more ſpirituall converſe, more agreeable to their owne nature, but ever they have bene beingh that have had and ſtill have, a great part to play, and therefore as the good Angells are of more uſe then wee conſider, ſo the evill (which is to our purpoſe eſpecially) are moſt powerfull and malignant ſubſtances, farre above the capacity of fleſh and blood, carrying themſelves rather as Princes and Powers, and Dominions, and being acted with the greateſt malice, are alwaies watching, alwaies tempting, alwaies obſerving, ever (if wee looke not to it) ruining and deſtroying us, warring with weapons ſutable to our complexions and luſts, betraying ſimple ſoules with

their

their methods and wiles, ſo as without a great power of God, wee ſhall not be able to eſcape them : The not conſidering of this enemy gives him a mighty advantage, wee hope in ſome meaſure to unmaſke him.

Wee have conſidered two things already concerning the nature of Angells in generall, firſt that they are creatures, ſecondly that they are ſubſtances and have made uſe of both : Wee ſhall now conſider their mutability, or immutability.

And firſt wee ſay that as it is peculier to God onely to be without beginning, ſo it belongs to God onely to be without change, or ſhadowe of change, and that the Angells as creatures are reduceable to nothing, by the ſame hand that made them, ſo as though there be no paſſive principle in them, by which they may be called corruptible, or mortall, yet in reſpect of an active power of God, upon which their being and life depends, they may be called corruptible, and mortall, becauſe as it is in the power of the Creator that things are, ſo it is in the power of the Creator that they may not bee, yea ſo much they are in Gods hands, though the beſt pieces of nature, that if hee doe but withdrawe his hand, they all moulder to nothing, there neede no great activity be put forth, a meere ceaſing to uphold them is ſufficent to deſtroy them; but yet when yee ſpeake of changeable or corruptible, it muſt be underſtood of the next and intrinſicall cauſe, and not of the remote and outward cauſe, as men are not called the children of the *Sunne*, though *Sol & homo generat hominem*, but of their parents, ſo as the Angells may properly be called incorruptible and immortall, becauſe they are ſo by nature; I ſpeake not now of the changeableneſſe of their wills, but of their nature and ſubſtance, the reaſons are.

Firſt

First because the Angells are not produced out of **1.**
the power of any matter as corporall substances, and
the soules of beasts, but are produced onely by the word
of God, and therefore as they have no internall principle of being, so have they none of dissolution, for
there is the same reason of being, and not being.

Secondly Angelicall natures as the soules also of men, **2.**
are not compounded of matter & forme, but are simple
formes and substances, subsisting by themselves; now
all corruption, mortality, and death is by the separation of the forme from the matter, as when the soule
is separated from the body, which is corruption, or
death, or when the accidentall forme is separated from
the subject, as white from the wall, or health from the
man, now what ever wants matter is incorruptible,
because there is no composition, and so no separation;
but the Scripture concludes this best in assimulating
the state of immortality in which wee shall be to the
Angells; This is the third consideration wee make of
the nature of Angells, that they are immutable.

Fourthly wee will consider of the apparitions of **4.**
Angells, of which wee heare so frequent mention in
the Scriptures, and the consideration whereof will
proove so proper to our purpose.

One manner of their appearings hath bene in
dreames, another in visions, the third in assumption
of bodies, and that either of bodies formed of nothing,
or of pre-existant matter them formed, or possessing
and acting naturall bodies already made.

Some have thought, there hath bene no assumption
of bodies, but onely an appearance to the fancy and
imagination; but that must needs be otherwise, for
what ever is a substance which is not a body, nor hath
a body naturally united, and yet is sometime seene

B 3 with

with a bodily fight or vifion muft needs take up a body, and further this was not an imaginary and phantafticall apparition, becaufe fuch an imagination is not feene by the fences without, but by the fancy within.

2.   2. An imaginative fight being onely within in the imagination confequently appeares to him onely, which fo fees it, but that which is feene by the eyes, becaufe it exifts without and not within the minde, may be feene alfo of all others fuch apparitions, were of the Angells that appeared to Abraham, to Lott, and to the men of Sodome, who were feene by them, and indifferently by all.

Obj.   But if you object to what end was this affumption of bodies, fince the power of the Angells exceeds all bodily might (and this will not be unufefull to confider fince it makes way to fhew to what end they appeare and what they have done, and can doe for us and upon us, both the good and bad.)

Anf.   The Angells affumed bodies for the manifefting themfelves, not for the doing of their worke; but that they might familiarly fpeake with men, without their terrour and dread. *Aquinas* gives other reafons, that they might manifeft the intelligible fociety and converfe which men expect with them in another life; And in the old Teftament that it was a certaine figurative declaration, that the word of God fhould take humane flefh, for all apparitions in the old Teftament were in order to that apparition of the fonne of God in the flefh: If you afke mee what kinde of bodies they tooke, and whether they were true men or no, in taking humane fhapes? Anfw. Firft though they appeared in a humane fhape, they were not true men, as Chrift was a true man, becaufe hee was perfonally and *hypoftatically* united; but bodies were not united

united to the Angells, as to their forme, as the bodie is to the soule which is its forme, nor was the humane nature body and soule, united to the person of any Angell, but they tooke bodies to them as garments which they tooke up, and laid downe upon occasion.

If you aske of what those bodies consisted? It is like ordinarily of some of the Elements, as of the ayre. And if you object that the ayre is improper to take figure or coulour, because it is so thin and transparent? The answer is, that although the ayre remaining in its rarity doth not reteyne figure or coulour, yet when it is condenced and thickened, it will doe both as appeares in the clouds. Another way of appearing was in possessing some naturall body, so the divell entred into the serpent, and an Angell spake in Balams Asse; so you read often of men possessed with evill Angells, the men spake not, but the divell in them, the like may be said often of the good.

Now if any shall aske what becomes of those bodies? The answer is, if they be created of nothing, they are reduced into nothing, by the power of God; But if they be formed of pre-existent matter, the worke being done for which they were taken up, they are resolved againe into their Elements, or Principles, but if the bodies were naturall, reall and existent before, they were left so againe, by the departing of the Angells, so was *Balams* asse and many bodies possest by the divells cast out by Christ.

Another consideration is whether the Angells having assumed those bodies, did put forth acts of life, whether they spake and sung, or eate and drunke, as they seemed to doe; this is handled with much controversie, but it is certaine they did what they seemed to doe, as appeares by the plaine direct story of Moses

con-

Qu.
Ans.

concerning the Angells, that appeared to Abraham, and others, and this is assur'd that what ever the Angells appeared to have, or doe, that they had, & did, for they never deceived your sences, their coulour, their shape, their eating, their drinking, their speaking was what it seemed to be, for the sences are not deceived about their objects, if the distance be proportionable, and they no way distempered, for if the sences are ordinarily capable of being deceived, then you may question any thing, subjected to sence, as whether the snow be whit, &c. Now all this they did, not by vertue of an internall forme, but an Angelicall power, quickening and mooving the body they acted; and it is observable, that when the Angells would hide their natures, that they might converse more familiarly with men, they would eate, and drinke, and speake; But when they would be acknowledged for Angells, then they denied to eate meate, as Iudges 6. in the story of *Gedion*, and of *Sampson*, Iudges 13. If you aske what became of the meate they eate, for their assumed bodies needed no nourishment? I would aske you what became of their bodies, their meate aswell as their bodies was reduced into nothing, or the preexistent Elements, of which they consisted, as that which Christ eate after his resurrection.

Qu.   There is one question more in this subject, with which I will end, and that is; Why the Angells make not their operations now, as formerly they have done?

Ans.   The heathen who were ignorant of the wayes of God, ascribe this to the sins of men, that God being now displeased with them, hath no more minde to converse with them; But the reason is quite otherwise, because as God would be worshipped in spirit and
truth,

truth, so hee would have us walke in the spirit, and converse more with the spirit then formerly, and Christ being now in the flesh, and in heaven, hee would have us live, by the faith of him, and a greater measure of the spirit being now given, hee would have us converse with the spirit, and these spirits, in a more invisible way : As also the Church being now confirmed by God, needs not those visible, and sensible confirmations, as formerly, which is the reason also of the ceasing of miracles, they were appropriated to the laying of fondations, both of the law and the Gospell, we walke now in the vertue of these apparitions, which were of old and in the power of these miracles, and besides wee have faith enableing us to converse with the Angells in a way more spirituall : So much for the apparition of Angells.

First from the immutability of the Angells, you see the reason of their indurance, nothing can destroy them, but God immediately, and God will not, the same reason is for the soules of men, for they as the Angells are not produced out of matter, are not compounded of matter and forme, but are pure substances, created and infused by God immediately, and so not subject to corruption : And for glorified bodies, when they shall have put on a celestiall forme, *this corruptible shall have put on incorruption*, this passive principle by which they are corruptible shalbe destroyed, they will then be in the same condition of the Angells, uncapable of fadeing or alteration.

From the apparition of Angells, see the care that God hath had of his Church in all times, *Hee hath not left himself without witnesse to the world, in that hee gave them raine and fruitfull seasons*, nor to his people, for hee hath given them the apparitions of Angells and invisible substances.

Coral.

1.

C   Secondly

2. 　　Secondly, learne the dignity of faints that have had the Angells to be their minifters, and fo farre as to humble and debafe themfelves to take up fhapes, that were not their owne, Heb. 1.14. *Are they not all miniftring fpirits, &c.*

3. 　　Thirdly, confider the meanenefle of mans nature in refpect of the Angelicall, wee cannot beare apparitions fcarce in our owne fhape, but out of it in any higher wee are confounded.

4. 　　Fourthly, fee the blefledneffe of our conditions, wee fhall be as the Angells, as little depending on Elements and outward things, the more wee can frame our felves to this independency of living now, the more raifed wee are, it is good to have our happines in few things, and to be eafily able to quit the reft.

5. 　　Fiftly, admire not bodily beauty, you fee an Angell which is a creature, but one degree above us can frame beautifull fhapes, which fhall be acted and moved and within a while comes to nothing, and this beauty of our bodies, this Elementary beauty, this mixture of whit and red, is almoft as perifhing, a little blaft of ficknes, a little undue commotion of the humours renders it alfo nothing.

6. 　　Sixtly, fee the great love of the fon of God in his apparition, who though above Angells, as being their creatour, Coll.1.16. *Though hee were God blefled for ever,* yet did not abhorre our nature, but as hee tooke our nature and not that of the Angells, fo hee tooke it up indeed, not in fhewe, as the Angells who troubled not themfelves, with the heavinefle, indifpofition, and vildenefle of our bodies, but Chrift fo tooke our nature, as he fubjected himfelfe to all our naturall infirmities, and to have as wee, a vilde body.

7. 　　Seaventhly, by the frequency of the former apparitions

tions

tions of the Angells, you may know they are not idle now, although wee living by faith have not such a visible converse with them as formerly, but as miracles are ceased, so are their appearings seased, but not their workings though their converse be not so sencible, yet it is as reall: But of that in another place.

So as the fifth thing will be to consider about the administrations of Angells to us, and the deputations they have from God concerning us.

And first, wee must know that the doctrine of the Angell Gardians hath bene exceeding antient, not onely amongst the Christians, but the heathens also, who drew much of their knowledge from the Scripture, and they thought that every man had his Angell, which was his *Genius,* hence are those phrases, *Invitâ Minervâ, & contra genui facere,* that when their Angell or *Genius* inspired them one way, they would do acts notwithstanding contrary to such inspirations, and to their *Genius.* **1.**

Secondly, some, not onely Philosophers, but Christians have thought that every man good and bad, was under the guidance of a good Angell, which to the reprobate was an aggravation of their sinnes, but it is cleare that the tutelage of the good Angells, belongs onely to the elect for so it is, Heb. 1. 14. *Are they not all ministring spirits, sent forth to minister to them who shall be heires of salvation?* Exclusively, that is, to them and no others. Els hee would not have made it a priviledge, and prerogative to the saints, but given it in common rather amongst men. So Psal. 91. 11. *Hee shall give his Angells charge over thee,* but to whome? ver. 9. *those which make the Lord their refuge,* so that it is cleare, for them and for no others. **2.**

And it doth not hinder, that this was spoken imme-

diately

diately to Chrift, for fo are all the promifes which concerne the elect, they are made, and made good firft to Chrift, and from him as a head they difcend to his members.

3.   A third confideration will be, whether every elect perfon hath a particular Angell deputed for him, or whether all indifferently ferve all: Not to trouble you with the difpute, fome incline rather to the negative, becaufe they thinke it is a derogation to the goodnes of God to his people, who gives them the heavenly hoft amongft them and to them all, for their ufe and protection, but neither doth this fatisfy mee, nor their anfwere to the places alleadged, for the former opinion, but before wee proceed further I affirme:

That it is probable that every elect hath his proper and peculiar Angell deputed as his keeper and companion, yet fo as extraordinarily many may be fent to his ayde, for proofe of this Math. 18. 10. *Take heed that you defpife not one of thefe little ones, for in heaven their Angells doe alwayes behold the face of my Father which is in heaven.* Wherein feemes to beheld out plainely the particular guardian-fhip of Angells, for hee faith, *their Angells,* that is, their particular Angells, els hee might have faid the Angells, which are not onely their Angells, but the Angells of all the elect with them, fo as hee feemes to have meant their particular Angells which were deputed to them as tutors and keepers, which becaufe it was a thing fo honorable to them, they ought not to be difpifed; the *Antients* were of this opinion; and therefore Ierome fayes upon this place; It is a great dignity of foules that every one from his nativity hath an Angell delegated for his keeper. Alfo Acts 12. 15. when the company with one accord affirmed that it was Peters Angell, that knocked, as a thing

thing notorious amongſt them that men had their particular Angell guardians; And from this opinion amongſt the Iewes aroſe that received and common opinion among the heathen, that every one had his Angell or *Genius:* Now no man affirmes or need affirme that upon occaſion there are not more then one deputed to the ſervice of an elect man (which may ſatiſfie them of the other opinion) for many Angells carried Lazarus into Abrahams boſome, and the Angell of God rejoyce over one ſinner that repents : Beſides more Angells then one brought Lott out of Sodome. As for the anſwere out of that place of Peter, that it might be one of his Angells, that lookes like an evaſion, nor ſeemes it any derogation, but an honour to the ſaints to have their particular Angells, ſo as wee doe not limit them to one, in all caſes; About this there are ſome other queſtions mooved; As when this Angell Guardian begins his charge, whether when the child is borne, or baptized, or afterwards. There is no reaſon why the beginning ſhould depend upon Baptiſme or any ordinance; for the other if one would argue it there might be more queſtion, I ſhould rather thinke that the Angells begins the execution of his charge, aſſoone as the ſoule is infuſed, for though the child be a part of the mother, yet it hath a diſtinct being of his owne, and is a perſon conſiſting of ſoule and body: Againe ſome conſider whether the Angell keepers doe ever leave men or no with whoſe Guardianſhip they are be truſted? Certainely never totally, for as our adverſary the divell goes about ſeeking whom hee may deſtroy, ſo our Angells intend their worke, of preſerving and keeping with all diligence; But as God leaves us that affliction or ſin may follow : So may the Angells of God alſo, which are his meſſengers and

C 3   mini-

ministers, they may withdrawe for a time of affliction and the like, and returne againe for our advantage: for the keeping of the Angells is nothing els, but a certaine execution of Divine providence concerning us; Now God never leaves us, therefore not the Angells, But they are often with us as Phisitians are with those who have filthy ulcers, they stop their noses, & administer the medicine, so doe they, our vanity & sins extreamely offend them, as it doth God, yet their obedience to God and Love to us, keepes them steddily to us, though in our ill waies, wee are no waies pleasant to them, but *They shall alwayes beare us in their armes*, as Psal. 91. that no evill befall us.

Qu. The next Question as an Appendix of this is, whether Provinces, or Communities have their Angell Guardians or no: It is very probable they have, as men their particular guardians, and yet the concurrence and assistance of more as they need, that place of the 10. of *Daniel* is famous where mention is made of the Prince of the Kingdome of Persia, and of the Prince of Grecia, and of Michael their Prince ver. 20. 21. and ver. 13. *The Prince of the Kingdome of Persia withstood him, but Michael their Prince came to helpe him:* Upon this place so cleare Ierome, and all expositours agree, that there are Angells deputed to the care and protection of *Provinces & Countries*, some other places are brought, but this cleare one shall suffice; The same reason also might be given for Churches which are Communities very deare unto God; The fathers were of that minde, and many bring those places of the *Revelation* to the Angell of particular Churches, as of *Ephesus, &c.* which they understood of the Angell Guardian; I will not dispute that, but that place of 1. Cor. 11. 10. might mee thinkes as probably be urged, where the women were to have
power

power over their Heads, becaufe of the Angells, in which place certainly the *Angells*, not the Minifters, are meant. And me thinkes it is *pro ratio* or an argument rather from the leffer to the greater, God doth take care for oxen, faith Paul, then much more for Minifters; So doth God give fuch honour to *Provinces*, then much more to Churches, which are Communities much dearer to him, but I fhall not enlarge this now particularly.

Wee will now fpeake of the reafons, why God ufeth this miniftry of Angells towards us.

If you afke in generall why God ufeth the miniftry | *Qu.*
of Angells? It is for his owne glory, hee hath creatures about him fit for his fervice, *Dan.* 7. 10. there is a brave Court, *Thoufand*, *Thoufands minifter unto him, and ten thoufand times, ten thoufand ftand before him.*

But if you afke, why God ufeth this Miniftration | *Qu.*
and Guardianfhip of Angells, towards us?

Hee doth it firft to preferve that Eutaxy that good | *Anf.* 1.
order, which hee hath put into things, as thicker bodies, and more inferiour are managed by more fubtile and powerfull; So the Bodies of the Beafts by a fpirit of life, and irrationall fpirits by rationall, as Men governe Beafts, fo by the fame reafon of proportion, the Angells which are invifible fpirits, and are all fpirits, have an influence upon men, which are partly fpirits and partly bodies. Thus the Fathers, all vifible things are moderatedly invifible, which what can it be els under God, fay they, but the Angells and fpirits of juft men, becaufe things muft be governed by that which is higher and purer then it felf; So that as God in refpect of the earth and fruits of it, places the Heavens next him, *I will heare the Heavens*; So in this fubordination, Angells comes next to have an influence upon rationall creatures.

Secondly,

2. Secondly, God doth it for our very great comfort
and confolation, what a happines is it that a haire of
our heads *cannot fall to the ground without* Gods notice,
that *they are all numbred, that God knowes and mindes all
our wayes*; but now when God fhall raife up fuch powers
for us, when wee fee the chariots and horfes, this addes
to our courage and affurance as it did to Iacobs, God
hath faid hee will never leave us, nor forfake us: But when
wee fee corne and wine, when wee fee him compaffing
us about with meanes futable to our neceffities, this
confirmes us, as being a helpe proportionable to our
neede, wee fee our good and our defires, not onely in
the remote caufe, but in the next and immediate. God
hath formed the Angells, for the effecting many great
workes about us and upon us, though wee little confider
it; now when wee fee mighty creatures, fitted for thofe
fervices, wee ought to have ftrong confolation, but the
Angells are framed miniftering fpirits, Heb. 1. 14. God
indeed doth all things, yet hee fpeakes by men, and teacheth alfo by his fpirit, & there is a forme above men,
Angells, which hee ufeth alfo, they *beare us in their armes,
and pitch their tents about us*, and doe much for us.

3. Thirdly God ufeth the Angells for their good and
honour, whom hee vonchfafeth to ufe as fellow-worke-
men with himfelfe and his fon; this was Pauls honour
that hee wrought together with God; Now the Angells which are deare to God are ufed in great imploy-
ments, as God is wont to ferve himfelf of thofe hee
loves to fome imployment or other.

4. Fourthly that there may a love and acquaintance
grow betweene us and the Angells, with whom wee
muft live for ever, and whom wee muft be like: Now
love growes by mutuall offices, as is feene in the love of
mothers to their children, which increafe by foftering
and tending on them.   Its

Its good to be a Saint, that yee may have the tutelage of Angells, *This honour have all the faints*, and none but they.

The wicked have no Angells to looke to them, to take care of them particularly, though they may fall perhaps under fome generall charge and care, as they doe alfo of God, that they may be preferved to their condition. God takes care of them fo farre, and fo may the Angells, but they are properly Guardians and miniftering fpirits to the faints, they are particularly miniftering fpirits *to the heirs of falvation.*

Its good to be a Church for the fame reafon, there being to Churches a fuperadded deputation to that of Saints, for to Churches alfo Angells feeme to be deftined, to which purpofe that place mentioned before is not inconfiderable, 1 Cor. 11. 10. *becaufe of the Angells,* on which place Peter Martyr fayes, wee ought to thinke that they have a care of our Churches afwell as of the Iewes, for fayes hee, it is faid Dan. 12. that Michael the Prince ftood for the children of Ifrael, and that this place is meant of the Angells and not of the Minifters, you have alfo the authority of Calvin, who obferves the word Angell is never appropriated to Minifters, without fome addition, as *to the Angell of Ephefus, &c.* befides

2.

There would have bene more reafon to have faid, that the women fhould have had power of their heads in refpect of their hufbandes, or the whole congregation, then the Minifters onely, and to improove this further, let this confideration worke upon you, leaft the Angells be provoked to withdraw, as I told you they would, this is common to Churches and Chriftians both, for as the holy Angells rejoyce at the converfion of a finner, and in our right order, fo

D they

they are offended and chaſtice according to their com-
miſſion given them from God, when wee doe otherwiſe.

3.   Thirdly that ſince the happines of theſe bleſſed Angells lies in working as it doth, for it was given as one
reaſon of their charge, *that they might worke with him*,
ſo ours alſo, and though the ſervices wee are imployed
in may ſeeme much belowe us, yet if they be Gods,
and in reference to that order hee ſets in the world and
much more, if they be in order to the ſaints and their
good and advancement, then be not aſhamed of the
ſervices which Angells performe, and be not weary of
working which is the beſt improvement of the holy
Angells.

4.   Fourthly let us ſo walke both as Chriſtians and
members of Churches, that the Angells may diſcharge
themſelves of their worke with joy and not with
griefe, for that will be unprofitable for us.

Thus you ſee in generall their charge you are fairly
weited on, you have particular Angell Guardians, and
in caſe of need you may have whole legions.

Next wee will come to conſider of their power over
our bodies and mindes, where it will be requiſite to
conſider firſt of the knowledge they have of things,
after of the excerciſe of their power, and then proceed
to the evill workings of the evill Angells, which is
that principally intended.

Wee have already made this corrolary, that wee
ſhould ſo walke as the Angells might diſcharge themſelves with joy at the laſt day; But that which ſeemes
to be the proper uſe of the foregoeing point, is, that
wee ſhould leade heere Angelicall lives, if the Angells
guard us and accompany us, wee ſhould ſavour of
their converſe : Men are knowne by their company,
they

they are not idle attendants, such as great men have for a parade and a shew, nor is their speciall influence upon our outward man, as wee shall shew hereafter, mee thinkes wee should not keepe such company in vaine, but should savour of a spirituall abstracted communion, that as they tooke bodies to themselves in their apparitions, not for any pleasure they had in them, but for our need; so wee should use outward and bodily things for the needs of the bodies, and should please our spirits and the good Angells with whom wee converse, and who are about us, by gaining ground, as much of the flesh and corruption as is possible, and bring the body as neere as may bee into a spirituall frame by possessing it in sanctification and honour, and by making it serviceable to our minde, using it, and not being used and commaunded by it; This will gratify the good Angells which the Scripture expects at our hands, 1. Cor. 11. 10. But this onely by way of addition to what was said before.

That wee have next to speake of, is the power of the Angells, then, how it is excercised and put forth towards us.

And because a great peece of their abilitie lies in their knowledge, wee will confider that:

That they are indued with an excellent knowledge, as being the highest of all intellectuall creatures, is without all question, and will appeare in confidering what their knowledge is.

And first Auften and the school-men, which follow him, give unto the Angells a knowledge which they call *Cognitio matutina & vespertina*, a morning and evening knowledge, or a day or a night knowledge.

They call that the morning knowledge, which respects the things in its cause, and that the evening knowledge which refpects the things in its effects, the one is a cleare knowledge, the other obfcure.

So as the morning or cleare knowledge is, that by which the Angells fee all things in the warde, that is in the funne by whom they were created; The evening or darke knowledge, is that by which they fee the fame things in themfelves or in their owne natures.

As the knowledge of a line or circle, by a Mathematicus defcription, is a right knowledge in the beauty and proportion of it, but the knowledge of it as made in the duft, is to know it with many imperfections.

But the knowledge of the Angells may be diftinguifh't either into a naturall knowledge, of which in a great meafure the good and ill were partakers, for fo it is faid, that fome ftood in the truth, and others fell from the truth, Joh. 8. 44. *Hee was a murtherer from the beginning, and abode not in the truth.* Therefore there was a truth and knowledge which fome adhered to and fome not.

2.   The fecond is by revelation, fo to the Angell in Daniel was revealed the miftery of the 70 weekes, fo the Angell revealed to Iohn the things hee knew not before, and of fuch things are they the meffengers to the fonnes of men.

3.   A third is by experience, fo they fee the manifold wifedome of God in the Church, and this is of great ufe to the good, and evill Angells, for the fame way men have to grow wife they have alfo.

4.   A fourth is a fupernaturall knowledge, with which the elect Angells were indued, not in the creation, for then it would have bene a naturall knowledge, but afterwards : And this anfwers a great objection, why fome Angells ftood and fome fell, when as they all

fawe

ſawe God; and, I have formerly in another diſcourſe
affirmed, that when wee ſhall ſee God face to face, it
will be impoſſible to ſinne, or to turne away from that
viſion. The truth is, the reprobate Angells never ſaw
God, as the elect did, for the will of the good Angells
would never have bene firmer, if their underſtanding
had not bene other wiſe enlightened, for it is the light
of the underſtanding that hath the great influence
upon the will, as wee ſee, ſo wee effect and moove. Now
of the elect Angells it is ſaid, *that they alwayes behold*
the face of the Father, which of the reprobate is not ſaid;
now yee know what it is to ſee God face to face, that
is, to ſee him evidently, clearely, as hee is to be ſeene,
without a ſtraitened and modificated viſion, which is
the great happines of men : You ſee now what kinde
of knowledge the Angells have, the laſt of which,
namely ſupernaturall, was peculiar to the elect Angells,
and ſtood them in ſuch ſteade as it kept them from
falling away, when others fell to their owne perdition.

If you aſke mee how, or in what manner the Angells
know ? Wee muſt conſider, how wee our ſelves know,
wee know a thing as wee ſee it, for the eye of the body
hath a kinde of reſemblance to the eye of the minde,
now to ſeeing there is required firſt a power of ſeeing
in the eye. Secondly a light through which wee ſee, if
the eye be blinde, or there be a hurt or wound in it,
that there be not a facultie of ſeeing, you ſee not
though you have light, and there muſt be light aſwell
as an eye, or you ſee not neither. Thirdly the ſpecies
or image of the thing you ſee, this altogether makes
viſion; So in the underſtanding there is in like manner
the power of the underſtanding, by which wee are
made able to judge, then a light by which the minde is
enlightened to perceive its object, and then the ſpecies

or image of the thing, out of the understanding, by
which the thing is made present to the understanding.
The two first are common to us with the Angells, to
wit, the power of knowing, and the light by which
wee know, they know more, but the way is the same.
The question is onely of the last whether they understand as wee, by species or images received from
things or otherwise; It is certaine they know not all
things by their owne essence, as God doth, for God
containes all things in himselfe, and is himselfe the
likenes and copie of all other things, and therefore
knowing himselfe as hee doth most perfectly, hee
knowes every thing, els of which hee is the copie:
Somethings they know by their owne essence, as the
eye sees the light by it self, not by any image of it; so
the Angells know themselves, by their owne essence,
but of things without them, they know them by
species, and representations not which they take of
from the things, but such as are put into them, by
God; Wee take of the image of God first by our
outward sences, as the eye takes of the image, of
what ever it sees, then by our fancy, and lastly wee
forme a kinde of intelligible species sutable and proportionable to the things wee would know: But the
Angells, which have not either outward or inward
sences, have not this way of knowing things, and
therefore know them by species put into them by
God.

One thing more is considerable, that is, whether the
Angells know by reasoning and dividing and com-
pounding as wee know, by drawing consequences,
from principles already acknowledged.

It is certaine they apprehend things quickly, as appeares by the comparison of a learned and wise man,

with

with one who is not ; give a wife man any ground or principle, hee will make out of that many conclufions : So in matters of numbring and account; an accountant will tell you that in a quarter of an hower, that another would be a day about. And though they doe know things by the effects, and by reafoning, yet it is with that quicknefle and certainty, that our greateft under-ftanding is darkneffe to it.

Another queftion is whether the Angells know particular things, and what ever is done heere ?

First, it is granted that they know one another fo as there is no Angell in heaven, which is not knowne by his fellow ; Without which they would not enjoy one another, and fo not be leffe happy : Even as wee fhall know the enumerable company of Angells, and the fpirits of juft men, nor is there any Divell in the ayre, or feas, or under the earth, which the good Angells know not, for how could they els refift them, on our behalfe.

Secondly, it muft needs be granted that the good Angells know not onely the feverall kindes and fpecies of things, the humane nature, and all the kindes of creatures in heaven, and earth, and fea, with their properties and natures perfectly and exactly, (for men in a great part know thefe things, how much more powers fo much fuperiour) but alfo they know particular things, that as God knowes all things by one image and likenes, which is his effence, (which is the efficient, finall and exemplary caufe of all things,) fo the Angells by thofe many univerfall fpecies, which are put into them by God, know not onely univerfall, but fingular and particular things, for as any thing is more raifed, and excellent, fo it hath its ftrength and power more united, and is more efficatious, and there-fore

fore with their underftanding onely by the univerfall
fpecies of things put into them by God , they know
thofe things, which men take in, by their many fences,
outward and inward , to wit , particular and fingular
things.

But now whether the Angells know all the particular actions , what ever is done , faid , or fuffered , is
more queftionable ; Of thofe committed to their
charge there is no queftion , but to affirme fo of all ,
and all at once , were to intrench to much upon Gods
priviledge , to whom and to no other all things are
open, and naked, there is to much of infinity in that.

As for our thoughts , affections, and defires , they
know them either by revelation , or externall fignes.
For God is onely the fearcher of the hearts , *Thou*
onely knoweft the hearts of the children of men. But they are
extreamely ingenious in gueffing , if Phifitians, by the
pulfe and temper can tell your affections and paffions,
as that you are in love or take care, if a wife man, or
an acquaintance can do any thing this way, they much
more.

Corol.

1.

Firft obferve that in this vaft compaffe of the Angells knowledge, and the feverall kindes of it , it was
fupernaturall knowledge that ftood them in the
greateft ftead , the other perifhed with them , it was
the beholding of the face of God , that filled them
and poffeft them , that tied them faft to God , that
wrought effectually upon their wills , the other Angells that had all the other forts of knowledge in the
largeft compaffe of it , carried it to hell with them ,
and the fame difference of naturall and fupernaturall
light, is feene amongft us every day; why doe the poore
receive the Gofpell and Chrift , *in whom are hid all the*
treafures of wifedome and knowledge , when the wife and
knowing

knowing men caſt it far from them ; Its certain this
is the greateſt wiſedome in the world to take Chriſt,
to make ſure of another life, this is wiſdome, and every
other thing in compariſon, is folly ; but whence hath
this poore man wiſdome and others not ; but becauſe
they ſee nothing of God after a ſupernaturall way,
they ſee God in a proportion, as the divells ſaw God
before the fall; there wants life, there wants fire, there
wants a touch in what ever they ſee, that would improove all, that would render all the reſt efficatious :
The ſame ſermon that ſpeakes to the reaſon onely of
one man, ſpeakes to the heart and conſcience of another : It is a goodly picture to others, but it wants life,
they looke upon it with pleaſure, but they will never
fall in love with it ; They will never eſpouſe it, or as
wee told you, they ſee the circle in the duſt, but the
beauty and proportion, which is the tempting thing,
that they ſee not ; Pray therefore for ſupernaturall
light, that will improove all the reſt, and all the reſt
without it, will but helpe to render you inexcuſable,
and ſo leave you.

Secondly, ſee the ground of the firmeneſſe of your
condition in the next life, you ſhall be as the good Angells, you ſhall ſee the face of God, and then you are
ſure, your eyes nor hearts can never turne away from
that viſion. 2.

Thirdly, yee ſhall know what they know, and as
they know it, whence you ſee what raiſedned of your
conditions will bee. 3.

Fourthly, ſee how exceedingly you are expoſed to
the knowledge of the Angells. 4.

Now having conſidered of the knowledge of the
good Angells, in which a great part of their ability
lies, wee come to ſpeake of their power, and firſt upon
corporall things.　　　　　　　　　　E　　　　　　It

It is certain they can doe any thing which nature can doe, either mediately or immediately; for example, They can moove the heavens, they cannot make them ſtand ſtill, for that is againſt nature, they can kill men, but they cannot raiſe them from the dead.

Miracles they cannot worke unleſſe as Gods inſtruments, as in the mooving of the water in the poole of *Betheſda*, and gathering together of the dead at the day of judgement.

God onely doth wonderfull things: Now a miracle is not that which is againſt the order of ſome particular nature, for then the flinging of a ſtone upwards were a miracle, but that is a miracle which is againſt the order of nature in generall, as if a ſtone of it ſelf ſhould moove upward, without any force or draweing.

So as the dividing of the Red-ſea was a miracle, and attributed to God onely, but the killing of the firſt-borne was none, and therefore attributed to an Angell; So the ſtanding ſtill of the Sun was aſcribed to God: But the victory they got Ioſhua 5. 15. to the Angell.

Againe, they doe ſome things immediately, as the killing of the whole army of Senacherib, and bringing Peter and the Apoſtles out of priſon. So they can moove all corporall things almoſt in an inſtant; they can ſtirre tempeſts; moove waters and windes, but other things they cannot doe immediately, as generation, &c. Nor can they do any thing as God, properly in an inſtant, and at their becke, as God and Chriſt, but either by locall motion or naturall medimus, though with an inconceiveable dexterity, and quicknes.

Laſtly all this power is ſubjected to the will of God, for ſo yee have it, *Bleſſe the Lord all yee Angells which are mighty*

mighty in strength, which do his will, Psal. 103. so *Thy will be done in earth as it is in heaven,* that is, as it is done by the Angells; So God sent his Angell and delivered Peter, Acts 12. 17. so saith Christ, *Could I not have asked my Father, and hee would give mee 12 Legions of Angells?* For their power over us, over our bodies, it is the same which they have over other things bodily. As for our outward sences they have great power over them, and that either by forming new objects, so in the 2. Kings 7. 6. *The Lord caused a sound of many horses to be heard,* by the army of the King of Assiria, which put them to flight. So the Angells tooke fiety bodies, 2. Kings 6. 17. *The mountaines were full of horses and chariots of fire.*

Againe, they can make such a commotion of the humours, within our bodies, that many things may appeare without which are not; They can also shut up the sences, as to the men of Sodome, Gen. 14. who were strucke with blindenesse.

As for the internall sences, to wit, the fancy and imagination, they have also a great power over them, as appeares by their appearing in dreames and visions; for in sleepe, our externall sences are so bound up, as wee discerne nothing by them; now wee being awake can by an act of our owne wills stirre up the memory of things and provoke our fancies, to the apprehension of things past. An Angell therefore can doe this much more, for what an inferiour power can doe, that a superiour can much more doe. Doe wee not see impressions in our fancy of things wee thought wee had altogether forgotten, which certainely is done by the Angells good and bad, which can make compositions of what they finde there, they cannot put in new ones, but worke upon what matter they finde.

As for their power over our underſtandings , and
wills this to mee is evident, that the great workes they
have to doe upon us, is upon the inward man, and that
being miniſtering ſpirits , their miniſtration is ſpirituall , and as the Divells, who though they doe ſome
things to our bodies, doe ever infect our ſpirits; ſo the
good Angells much rather apply themſelves in their
miniſtrations to our ſpirits , but to ſhew how they
can operate upon our underſtandings and wills, wee will
firſt lay this downe.

That God can onely , effectually enlighten the
underſtanding , and determine the will , hee can bend
and turne , and forme it , which way hee pleaſeth ; But
the Angells can ſpeake alſo , to thoſe pure ſpirituall
parts, & their ſpeaking carries a power with it, though
God onely determine : Firſt as one man teacheth
another, ſo the Angell ſpake to the bleſſed Virgin , by
apparition, by voyce ; Sometimes by voyce without
apparition , ſometimes by writing , ſo to Balteſhazer
by writing upon the wall , but they can inviſibly alſo
enlighten us , as appeares plainely in dreames , for ſo
they ſpake to Ioſeph in a dreame, Math. 1. and to many
others ; Now there is the ſame way and the ſame
reaſon , of ſpeaking to us waking and ſleeping : To
underſtand this, (and heerein the miniſtration of Angells to our ſpirits will appeare) wee muſt conceive
firſt , that the phantaſmes of things , received by the
outward ſences, are kept, and preſerved by the inward
ſences, or its organ , and inſtrument , as the ſpecies of
ſounds, of ſhapes, or what ever els : Secondly that theſe
phantaſmes ſo kept , may be ſo mooved , by ſome ex-
trinſecall thing, as they may move the fancy, and provoke it to repreſent and conceive more things and
divers , which neither appeare , nor are at that time
percei-

perceived, by any sence, this appeares evidently; Wee
can sit in the darke, where wee heare and see nothing,
and multiply a fancy in *infinitum*, by an act of our owne
will: Also without our will, this often appeares, as in
dreames. Now this inlarging, alteration and composition, must be by some motion of the subject in which
these fancies are, as also by a certaine motion of our
humours, and spirits. The fancy or imagination is
stirred up to the making of various apprehensions and
representations of things, this wee finde in dreames
which follow often the temperature of the body, as
appeares to every man, that hath in the least observed
himselfe; Also in sicknesses, which altering the bodie
and the humours, and so troubling the fancy, begets
strange fancies, and makes dreadfull, and fearefull representations to us, sometimes extreamely foolish,
as that which falls out as it were by chance, and by an
undue jumbling of things together; Now this know,
as wee saide before, that what ever an inferiour power
can doe, that a superiour can much more doe, such
fancies as befalls us (as it were) by chance, as in dreames
or sicknes, by casuall, inordinate, or naturall motion
of the humours, that the Angells especially the good
can most orderly and most efficaciously move, because
they doe what they doe from will and counsell, and
know exactly how the spirits and humours must be
mooved, that the phantasmes may be conveniently
applied to some conceptions or apprehensions, most
accommodate and fitted for the knowledge, of what
truth they would suggest.

Againe an Angell can remoove the impediments of
apprehension, as it lies in any commotion or pertur-
bation of the spirits, or the humours, an Angell can
helpe it, and the impediment shall cease, or if the organ

be

be to much intended, an Angell can in a great meafure accommodate and believe it.

Now of how great moment this is, to the enlightening of our underftandings, and mooving our wills, all men know, that have minded, that the underftanding receives things by the mediation, firft of the externall fences, then of the fancy, of which the memory is the treafurer, fo as all comes in to us this way, fo that to mee heere is the difference, betweene the converfe of men and Angells, men can fpeake to our underftandings by the mediation of our externall fences, Angells which are fpirits goe a neer way to worke, and fpeake to the internall, firft of all, making fuch compofitions there, as the underftanding prefently takes of, and reades what is written; As on the other fide, the underftanding imprints much upon the fancy what it conceives, there is fuch a neere relation betweene the body and the minde. Befides this way of writing in our fancies, almoft what they will, and fo fpeaking to us, by which they reprefent objects to our underftandings, and our wills which often take and moove us (as the objects of truth, or the appearance, hath a great power upon the underftanding, and the object of good upon the will) befides this, they can moove thofe fenfitive paffions which are in us; Anger concupifcence, which often moove us to chufe, to command, to will, and like *Sophifters* deceive us with the coulour of good, as wee finde by experience, and fee in Peter and David, and all the Saints.

Corol.
1.

Firft confider how great a knowledge the Angells have of us, how great an advantage upon us, there is fuch a linke betweene the body, and the minde, that to be well acquainted with a mans outward actions, to have a perfect experience of a mans difcourfe and actions,

actions, is almoſt to know him all; But how many inward motions are there, which never come to the view, how much boyling of the blood, to luſt, to revenge, that never appeares in the face, that the Angells know by beholding the interiour ſences, much more apparently then wee ſee it in the face; Beſides if it come to gueſſing what was the meaning of ſuch a looke, ſuch a motion, ſuch a bluſh, ſuch a paleneſſe, there wiſedome heere helpes them exceedingly, ſo as they are rarely deceived, beſides that as our thoughts are more in the fountaine then our actions, ſo the impreſſion upon our fancie is greater then upon our face, which our feare or wiſedome often keepes in. Thus much for their knowledge and light of us, which you ſee how great it is: Then for their power upon us, almoſt what can they not doe upon our bodies, upon our ſences outward and inward, upon our mindes, for by the meanes I have told you, what is it that they cannot communicate to you at their pleaſure, ſpeaking to the inward ſences, and cauſing the underſtanding to reade of, what they there compound, and no time is free ſleeping and waking, they can come to you, when the ſences are bound up, as in dreames, they need not fetch the compaſſe of our eares, and eyes, that wee are faine to doe, therefore our communion is exceeding great with the Angells, both good and bad; For (beleeve it) they having ſuch a price in their hands, will not looſe it on either ſide, the Divells malice will not ſuffer them, nor the good Angells love and duty, will not ſuffer them to be wanting to their abilities, *Hee maketh his Angells ſpirits, his Miniſters a flame of fire,* this ſay ſome is with relation to their workeing toward us, both in lightening and heating; This is therefore firſt by conſidering the advantages they have

upon

upon us , to confider how great and intimate our converfe is with them; fecondly to confider this notwithftanding , that wee give not that which is Gods due
to the Angells , though they be *the beginning* of his
creation, for firft God onely knowes the heart, even our
thoughts afarre of , the Angells onely as I have told
you.

2.   Secondly for working upon us , as all they doe is
under God, and in fulfilling his will, which is the law
and rule they moove by , fo they cannot put in new
fpecies of things into the fancy, and fuch as the fences
had never any knowledge of , though they can make
many compofitions and deductions , almoft to the
faying of what they will, yet their ability ftretches not
to the putting in of what was never there before , as
to make a man borne blinde , dreame of coulours and
their difference, therefore ,

3.   Thirdly , take heed of receiving ill impreffions by
your eares or your eyes , or any way , if an ill man
tell you an ill ftory once , the Divell will tell you it a
thoufand times , it is a great happines to this purpofe
not to know ill : And on the other fide , keepe your
felves in fuch a holy frame , as may provoke the good
Angells to converfe with you , wee love to fpeake
where wee are like to finde intertainement, and fo doe
they and receive good images and impreffions of
things, that they may have matter to worke upon, for
as I told you they cannot make a blinde man dreame
of coulours.

      Laftly for your foules fake keepe your body in a
good frame , that the humours of the body be not
armed againft you, to luft, and anger, and revenge, but
may be fitted for fpirituall converfe.

4.   Fourthly feare and pleafe God, who gives bounds to
the

the moſt raging elements, water, and fire, and to the
moſt mighty ſpirits the Angells, for they are his meſſengers, they doe his will; if you receive any good
motions or inſpirations, by the Angells, any thing of
comfort, it is God that doth it, hee commaunds that
creature aſwell as any other to give downe its milke,
therefore let him have the praiſe, and if now you will
offer a ſacrifice for this, offer it to the Lord, for ſo ſaith
the Angell himſelf, Iudges 13. 16. Revel. 19. 10.
Worſhip God (ſaith the Angell to Iohn:) *ſee thou do it not.*
The Angell had revealed great things to Iohn, and hee
would have worſhipped him, but ſaith the Angell, *ſee*
thou doe it not. Alſo 14. Rev. 7. *worſhip him ſaith the An-*
gell that made the heaven and the earth, and the ſea and the
fountaines of waters. But

Fifthly, love the Angells and gratify them, for they 5
love you and are mightily advantagious to you, they
love us much without all queſtion, for their wills are
as Gods will, and hee loves us and they know it, as being
deputed by him to miniſter to us: And as they themſelves love God above all, ſo they love us as themſelves,
which is the next commaund, for wee are their neighbours, they are very neere us, and wee ſhalbe much
neerer heareafter when wee ſhalbe with them, and be
as they are.

Laſtly, wee may ſee their love by its effects. Firſt 6.
by theſe workes for our good, they worke in us and
upon us, and then thoſe effects of love, they rejoyce
to looke into the good things prepared for us. 1. Pet.
1. 12. *which things the Angells deſire to looke into,* and as the
holy Spirit is grieved when wee ſin, ſo are the Angells
alſo, as appeares by their contrary affection of rejoycing at our good, and converſion, for then the *An-*
gells of heaven rejoyce. And therefore the Pſalmiſt pro-

F   vokes

vokes the Angells to praife God, for his mercies to
himfelfe and to us, and by the fame reafon that wee
hate the Divell, and refift him, wee fhould love and
gratifie the good Angells: They hate God, they hate
and tempt us, the others doe purely and truly the
contrary, let us know thefe fpirits, and grow into a
greater league and familiarity with them, let them
not have leffe of our love, becaufe they are fpirituall
and invifible, for that inables them to doe us more
fervice, and fo is God, whom wee love moft of all.

In this tract of Angells, that which moft immediately and particularly reatcheth my intent, is to
fhew the power they have over us, efpecially over
our fpirits, and the way they have to communicate
themfelves according to their power, efpecially to our
fpirits, which wee have done already, though other
things as a foundation, and in order to this were neceffary to be knowne, and particularly that about the
Guardian-fhip of Angells: From that formerly delivered wee deduced feverall corrolaries both from
the knowledge of the Angells, and from their power
of communicating it, to all which wee fhall onely adde
this further.

That they have not this knowledge and power in
vaine, but according to their talent betrufted with
them, they lay themfelves out for our advantage, as
concerning the outward man, fo efpecially and above
all, in relation to our fpirits and inward man, tacitely
and in a fpirituall way communicating themfelves to
our fpirits, fuggefting good things, and provoking us
to our duties in holines and obedience.

1.   This I proove, firft from their power, what they
can doe they doe, but they can communicate themfelves to our fpirits, and our inward man; they
                                                        can

can in a very great measure know our mindes and ne-
cessities, they can by the mediation of our fancies,
and inward sences speake to us, almost what ever they
will, therefore they doe it : The reason is cleare, for
els they should not serve God with all their might. But
wee told you before their obedience is the patterne
of ours, therefore their love also, and wee proved also
that they did love us exceedingly, because God loves
us, and as being their neighbours, therefore wanting
neither power to enable them to their duty, nor love
to actuate that power, and ability, they are no way
wanting to such a communion, without which as I have
shewed they should neither make good their love to
God, in serving him, with their strength, nor their
love to us in doeing us that good they are able to doe.

Secondly you may remember I told you, that they
did formerly take up their shapes, not for their owne
needs, but for ours, nor for ours to facilitate any thing
they were to effect upon us (for they could have communicated themselves, as much to us without bodies
as with) but for other reasons, as for the same, that
miracles were of use in the infancy of the Church, and
new establishment of religion, therefore what they
have done, they doe, for their ministery ceaseth not
though the way of their administration be changed :
Now to instance, they have in a more open and visible
way excercised themselves in communicating to us
spirituall things, the law it selfe the rule of all our
holines, and obedience, was given by the *Disposition
and ministration of Angells*, Acts 7. 53. Gal. 3. 19.

Consider those places a little, if any thing was administred by God immediately, one would thinke the
law was, yet heere it is plainely said, *ordained by Angells*, that is, the ministery of Angells was in it, perhaps

F 2 the

the voice that spake it was theirs, and so some thinke, for so Heb. 2. 2. *If the word spoken by Angells, was stedfast*, that is, the law, as for the Mediatour there mentioned, some understand it of Christ, others of Moses, but it is cleare that the law was promulged by God, by the ministration of Angells, and that though God be said to speake those words, it is *Elohim*, that is, the word used respecting his office as judge and supreame, and therefore the Angell that before sounded the trumpet, now sounded articulately the words, and whereas the phrase is God, spake, *these words*, that is, but according to the stile of Viceroyes, who write in their Masters name, *Charles King*.

And often in Scripture the word or action of the principall Agent, is ascribed to the Minister Timothie is said *to save himself, and those that heard him*. 1. Tim. 4. 16. *And the Saintes to judge the world*, who are but Ministers and approovers, for Christ is the great judge.

Obj. But God is so neere us, as hee should doe it himself, 1. Cor. 3. 16. *Know ye not that yee are the temple of God, and that the spirit of God dwells in you?* 1. Cor. 6. 19. *Know ye not that your bodie is the temple of the holy Ghost which is in you, &c.* These things are to be understood spiritually, (that is) wee are dedicated to God, as the Temple of God, and God is in us and among us by his spirit, there is no mention made of a personall union; so Christ Math. 18. 20. *Where two or three are gathered together in my name, there I am in the midst of them;* Yet notwithstanding hee is so neere us, hee doth not cease to teach us by the channells of ordinances. (Where by the way they administer no suggestion, but what is agreable to the word of God, which was given by them, for they will not contradict the rule, that themselves administred, and if any other be suggested, gefted, it is from the other kinde of Angells:) To proceede the Angell revealed to Mary the incarnation of Chrift according to the word Luke 1. And others in the fame chapter preacht the nativity of the Saviour of the world, fo Acts 1. they inftruct the Apoftles about the returne of Chrift to judgement, according to the word, alfo that God is onely to be worfhipped, Rev. 19. 10. And therefore Michaël contended with the Divell about the body of Mofes, that it might not be found and worfhipped: Not to be long, an Angell comforted Hagar, and admonifhed her of her duty, Gen. 16. So the Angell of the Lord comforted Paul, and all that was in the fhip with him, Acts 27. So an Angell ftrengthened and encouraged Eliah to his worke. 2. Kings 1. 3. In a word what ever by way of inftruction, of admonition, of incouragement, they have done in a way more vifible in the infancy of the Church, that they doe not ceafe to doe now, becaufe their miniftery remaines, though the way of their adminiftration, for reafons formerly mentioned, be altered.

A third reafon perfwading you to this may be that which the Divells doe on their part, they adminifter to our fpirits moft of all, their apparitions being almoft as feldome now a dayes as of the good Angells, they goe *about like roaring Lyons, feeking whom they may devour.* Their nets are alwayes fpread, they tende their fnares alwayes, not fo much for our bodies as our fpirits, as appeares by all manner of fpirituall temptations, carnall lufts are as much fpiritualized by them as may be; therefore the good Angells do the like, for their power is greater, and their love higher then the others malice.

Fourthly from their commiffion, Heb. 1. 14. is prooved their adminiftration efpecially to the inner

man,

man, they are miniftring fpirits, and what kinde of adminiftration that feemes to be, is excellently fet forth Pfal.91.11.12. *Hee fhall give his Angells charge over thee to keepe thee in all thy wayes, they fhall beare thee up in their hands, leaft thou dafh thy foote againft a ftone.* In this place the Angells are compared, firft to nurfes, or mothers, that have a charge over weake and infirme children, to keepe them and to guard them.

To carry them in their hands is a Metaphor, and fignifies a perfect execution of their cuftody, to have a fpeciall care of them, and therefore is rather expreft fo, then carrying them on their fhoulders, that which one carries on their hand they are fure to keepe; and the fpaniards have a proverb when they would fignify eminent favour, and friendfhip, they carry him upon the palmes of their hands, that is, they exceedingly love him, and diligently keepe him.

Leaft at any time, thou fhouldft dafh thy foote againft a ftone: Hee perfifts in the Metaphor; Children often ftumble and fall, unleffe they be ledd and carried in hands, and armes; by *Stones*, are meant all difficulties, objections, perills, both to the outward and inward man, as Chrift is faid to take care of haires and fparrowes, that is, of every thing even to a haire. Now wee know what this charge is faving that Zanchy addes alfo, the Metaphor of Schoolmafters, and fayes that wee are poore Rufticke people, ftrangers, but being adopted into the houfhold of God, hee gives his moft noble Minifters, the *Angells* charge, firft of our nurfing, and then of our education, when wee are weaned to inftruct us, to admonifh, to inftitute, to correct us, to comfort us, to defend us, to preferve us from all evill, & to provoke us to all good; And thefe Angells feeing that wee are fo deare to God, that for our fakes hee

fpared

spared not his owne Sonne, takes this charge with all their hearts upon them, and omit nothing of their duty from our birth to the end of our life.

And the same Zanchy sayes, that there be three speciall heads of the Angells working about us, the first is to preserve us, so far as God sees it profitable for us, from all the snares and force of the Divell, that they should be a watch about us, they should observe all our actions and carriages, both private and publique, taking care that no evill befall us. Secondly not onely this but especially that they should take care of our soules teaching us good things, declaring the will of God to us, revealing the misteryes of salvation, when hee pleaseth, taking care wee may be instructed in the law of God, which formerly they did in visions & dreames, as you have heard, now tacitely they admonish our mindes, and provoke us to good duties, to obedience, &c. Thirdly that in afflictions they comfort us, strengthen us, raise us, &c.

Bodin tells a story in his first booke of the history of Sorcerers of one who about the time of reformation of religion, desired much of God the guidance and assistance of an Angell, and from the 37 yeare of his age, hee had sensible manifestations of a spirit that assisted him, and followed him till his death; If in company hee chanced to speake any unwary words, hee was sure to be advertized, and reproved for it in a dreame in the night; if hee read a booke that was not good, the Angell would strike upon the booke to cause him to leave it: Also the Angell would usually wake him early and provoke him to prayer, and holy duties, hee was also ever forewarn'd of such accidents, as were to befall him, either for good or ill. Amongst others hee tells this particular story, that being to goe a journey by water, hee

hee was in extreame danger of his life, as hee knew afterwards, for some enemies of his, were resolved in the way to kill him, but the night before hee had a dreame that his father had bought him two horses, one red, another white, which caused him in the morning to send his servant, to hire him a couple of horses, which prooved to be of the same coulour red and whit, as hee had seene the vision in his dreame, although hee had spoken no words to his servant concerning the coulour; many other things hee mentions, very strang and considerable, but I shall inlarge this story no further nor adde any more, for the illustrating of this point.

So that you see this made good, that the Angells are of a mighty use to us, especially in a spirituall way, and to our inward man, that their administrations is not changed, but the way of it onely.

Obj.   But what doe wee leave now to Christ and the spirit, if you give to the Angells the worke of teaching and hinting spirituall things?

Ans.   I answere, what will you leave to the Angells, if you take this imployment from them, you will say bodily administrations, and what will you take away that from Christ, whose care reacheth to our bodies aswell as to our spirits, and to a haire of our heads. Therefore you have no such division of worke to make as to give to the Angells a care of the bodie to preserve from dangers, and to Christ the charge of the inner man, if it be no prejudice to Christ that the Angells take care of our bodies, which is also his care, what prejudice will it be that the Angells should also have a care of our spirits, unlesse you thinke it be a worke to high for them, and such as they cannot reach, but the contrary to that hath bene showne already, and wee finde

by

by woefull experience, that the Divells, whose power is lower then theirs, reach our spirits in their dayly temptations. But secondly I leave to Christ and the spirit the all in all, that is, the inspiration, the efficacy, and the blessing, for the Angells are but ministring spirits not fountaines, or heads of water, but cisternes and channells, it is Christ and the spirit that imploy the Angells, they give the blessing, and make effectuall what they doe : But you will aske what needs this administration, for Christ can doe this worke without them ? I aske aswell what needs Ministers, preaching, Sacraments, but because these are Gods wayes of administration, his ordinances of which wee can give no account, hee useth this chaine, and subordination of which one linke toucheth another, t'is Gods good pleasure to communicate himself to us, by meanes, and ordinances, of which the Angells are a great part, being a great ordinance of God to us, as effectuall but more inward, and the reasons why God useth the Angells towards us, I have largely given you.

Now if one should be so curious to consider what is by the immediate inspiration of God, to wit, what is done by God immediately, & what may the mediation of Angells and other ordinances ; were a search more vice then safe, as it would be also to distinguish what the Divell produceth upon us, by the mediation of our corruptions, or without them, though this latter may be more easily perhaps guessed at then the other, but there is no great use of it, and therefore wee will not amuse our selves, in giving an account of it; but this remaines a sure truth, that they are of mighty use to us, and that the things communicated to our inward man, is ordinarily the administration of Angells.

Then fight manfully the Lords Battailes, you see

Coroll.

G   not

not onely the fountain of your ftrength, and the
finifher of your faith, God and Chrift, but all the
intervening *Mediums*, the *Saints*, the *Ordinances*, and
another great ordinance in this kinde, we have not fo
much confidered, *the good Angells*, the chariots and
horfes fhould relieve us, as they did *Elifha*, and confider
this in relation to your religious walking, and to your
inward man, though you fhould want other ordinances,
yet yee have the Angells, an ordinance to walke up
and downe with you; in other things wee-judge it a
great matter to fee the meanes, to have befides the
promife the ftaffe of bread, and to other ordinances
alfo they are an addition, and improvement, confider
it alfo under this motion, that you may not be amafed
by beholding the Divell and our owne lufts, you have
not onely God, and Chrift, the Authour and finifher
of your faith, but you have this meanes alfo, a fpirituall
fubftance proportionable to the other, and to contend
with him in ftanding on their fide.

Secondly walke reverently in refpect of the Angells
even in your bedchambers, the prefence of the Angells
fhould hinder us from doeing that which it were
a fhame and difhonour, to be found doeing by men, and
fhould reftraine us even to our thoughts and fancies,
which they have a great ability to difcerne and finde
out.

Thirdly ufe meanes notwithftanding this ayde, the
Angells will helpe you *in all your wayes*, Chrift would
put them to no more, and when you have ufed other
meanes, then is their helpe moft feafonable; fo they
came and miniftred to Chrift after his conflict, after
hee had refifted the Divell, that is, then they comforted him, and applied fpirituall confolations, and if
to Chrift, then much more to us, their adminiftration

tion will be but in and with the use of meanes.

So as wee see the confideration of thofe blessed fpirits, is of a practicall influence, and is not onely for speculation, for what can be more availeable to us then to know all the channells and conduits through with God conveyes himfelf to us : Therefore every ordinance is fo pretious, becaufe it is a veyne or artery to convey blood, or fpirits from God, therefore wee fhould love them and reverence them, therefore wee converfe with them, and ftudy to know them, and finde them out, even the leaft peeces & circumftances of them, becaufe they convey fome thing of God, they are the pearles for which wee fell all wee have, to buy the field where they are to be found, they are our mines, our *Elixurs*, and our Philofophers ftone, turning all they touch into gold; therefore let us value the knowledge of them as things neceffary for us, and which have a great influence upon our holy walking.

And fecondly let us apply our felves to them, as to the ordinances, and Minifters of God, ufing them reverently, fucking good from them, confidering how wee may receive, what ever they adminifter, and becaufe thefe are rationall, and living inftruments, let us converfe with them, as fuch, knowing how to fpeake with them, knowing how to gaine them, and winne upon them, which is by living their lives, that is, according to reafon and the fpirit, anfwering them in their motions, converfing with them after a fpirituall way, affenting to what they fay, making up holy conclufions with them and replyes, which they will finde wayes to underftand, afwell as the Divell, as wee fhall heare afterward. And ufing things of fence as they did for ones, rather then their particular and perfonall fatisfaction.

G 2　　　　　　Thirdly

3.   Thirdly let us heere see, how all the whole creation
is serviceable to man, and reduceable to his good; The
beasts and plants feede and cloth him; The sun and
starres contribute to his being, food, and preservation,
they gouverne the yeare for the fruit, which hee gathers, and they have influence upon the humours, and
constitution of his body, the highest heavens is a house
prepared for him, to rest him in for ever, after a short
labour; one would have thought that if any peece of
the creation should have escaped this ministery, it
would have bene the mighty and blessed Angells, fitted
and destin'd for the ministery of the almighty God,
but behold them as farre engaged as any of the rest:
*What is man that thou art mindefull of him, or the Son of Man
that thou visitest him?* That is, with all thy mercyes and
blessings; now then this man that is thus waited on, by
the whole creation and by these mighty Angells, must
either put himself into the Throne of God, and thinke
that hee it is, to whom all these things doe homage,
as to their naturall and soveraigne Lord, as to their utmost and highest end, and this by nature wee would
faine doe: Or els hee must looke upon himself as a well
paid servant, as a well fitted instrument for some excellent and well raised worke, and that what ever
comings in hee hath, hee must consider them in order
to his layings out and his receipts to his disbursments;
Hee must consider the tract of obedience and the way
of working to which all this chaine, and charge of be-
nefite drive him, and must know that hee is the great
accountant of the world, both for talents the meanes
of working, and for wages the reward of working, and
should be fitted from every administration about him
to an answerable ministery in himself, with which hee
is charged, both in a way of love and debt; and for instance

ftance when hee knowes in this particular, that the
Angells continually adminifter good things to him,
inftructing, teaching, admonifhing him, infpiring
him with good, comforting, ftrengthening him
againft the Divell, and his lufts, hee is taught not
onely to receive willingly that which is fo freely and
advantageoufly adminiftred, and to love that God be
bove all, and then thofe fpirits, that are at this paines,
but hee is taught alfo to be good, to be holy, to be
ftrong, to let them have their efficacy upon him, to be
obedient, to make right pathes and fteppes. The fun
and the ftarres produce their effects upon the earth,
why fhould not the bleffed Angells and the bleffed
fpirits have their effects upon thy heart?

Laftly fince every ability and ftrength is for fervice,
why fhould not wee afpire after Angelicall worke, wee
have Angell Guardians, why fhould not wee be Guardians of one another, they teach us, why fhould not
wee inftruct the ignorant, that are below us either in
knowledge or grace; They comfort and ftrengthen
us, why fhould not wee doe the like; The way to have
Angells reward, to fee the face of God, is to doe the
worke of Angells, thofe infpired by the fpirit, are capable of Angells worke, afwell as of their wages. So you
will improove this piece of creation to your ufe afwell
as all the reft.

Wee come now to the fecond part of this Treaty
that of the Divell, and the evill Angells, where in wee
fhall handle fome things very briefly, and efpecially
infift upon thofe things, which are in relation to their
dealings with us.

And wee will confider them not as they were, for fo
their nature is common to them with the good Angells, but as they are.

G 3 If

If you aske, how they came into this woefull condition! Certainely by sin, for they were not so formed
by God; That they might sin, there is reason enough,
in this that they were creatures, for what is it to sin,
but to depart from that rectitude, which every thing
ought to have, to passe your bounds to decline and
erre from the scope appointed you, for Gods prerogative alone is to be immutable. That they did sin, the
Scripture is cleere, for *they left their first estate*, Iude 6.
and they aboade not in the truth. And 2. Pet. 2. 4. *God spared
not the Angells that sinned, but cast them into hell*. If you aske
what sin this was that brought those blessed creatures
into the depth of misery? the Scripture is not so cleare
in that, some thinke it was pride, and rebellion against
God, others thinke envy at man, the most probable
guesse mee thinkes is, that it was their opposition to
the great mistery of Godlinesse in the Gospell of
Christ, who being to be made man, and the head of all
the creation, that all standing, all restauration was to
be by God man, in which the Angelicall nature was
left out, this being in a great measure revealed as it is
called Rev. 14. 6. *The everlasting Gospell*, decreed from
eternity, though manifested but by degrees; those
high spirits could not beare such a subjection, so Christ
saith, *they abode not in the truth*, Ioh. 8. 44. especially
of the Gospell, which is the greatest truth in respect
of which Christ calls himselfe the *Truth*, and is
called *the wisedome of God*, so saith hee, *I came into this
world, that I might beare witnesse of the truth*; that is, this
truth, which Christ sealed with his blood, now sayes
hee, *hee abode not in this truth*, *but was a lyar*; now what
is that lye that Sathan sets up in the world, which hee
alwayes speakes, which hee studies to perswade others
to, it is this to debase the Gospell, and the saving of
                                                    the

the world by God man, and therefore its worth obſerving that the ſumme of al hereſies, are either againſt the divinity of Chriſt, or the humanity of Chriſt, or his office, to wit, that hee can contribute all things neceſſary to ſalvation, that his merits, his works alone, are enough : And in this reſpect Chriſt accuſed the Iewes, *you are the ſonnes of your father the Divell, which ſtood not in the truth,* no more will you, ſayes hee, but you lye as hee did : Now what was their lye, the very ſame, that Chriſt was not the Sonne of God, the Saviour of the world, and ſo the truth in which they would not reſt, was the truth of the Goſpell, which their father the Divell abode not in, and this is that truth which ever ſince hath beene the ground of the conflict betweene the good and evill Angells, and betweene the Divells, and the Saints of God.

See and tremble at the quicke worke that God made, 2. Peter 2. 4. *God ſpared not the Angells that ſinned, but caſt them into Hell;* hee might have dealt ſo with us, *the wages of ſin is death;* How come wee then to live, how comes it that wee are on this ſide hell, whither ſin would preſently have hurryed us, thanke God and Chriſt for it.

Coroll.
1.

Secondly, honour, love and beleeve the Goſpell, that is, the truth, the great truth, let up God and Chriſt greatly in it, beleeve ſtrongly, truſt not to your righteouſnes : Let not your ſinnes ſtand in your way, this coſt the Divells eternall condemnation; this is the truth they ſtood not in, this is the thing they moſt of all oppoſe. Therefore worke what you will, ſo you beleeve not, they care not, unbeliefe is virtually all ill, therefore fight eſpecially againſt that.

2.

Thirdly, feare ſins againſt great and ſtrong light, the Divells abode not in the truth, that truth they

3.

forſooke

forfooke was exceeding great, it was truth with a witneffe, exceeding evident, and apparent, therefore it carried them into the loweft finke of fin, which is a deadly hatred of God, and all goodnes, and all his creatures, which arifeth much from the light they fell from, like to this fall of theirs, is the fin againft the holy Ghoft. Having feene their fin, wee come to their punifhment, which in many refpects is neceffary for us to know in order to this fubject as wee fhall fee.

The place of their punifhment, feemes to admit of a double confideration, either that of their ultimate punifhment, after the day of judgment, or that for the prefent.

This diftinction is gathered out of feverall places, efpecially that of Iude; *That everlafting fire*, which Chrift fpeakes of Math. 25. 41. The common refidence of the Damned and Divells, feemes rather to be prepared for them, then poffeffed already by the Divell and his Angells: The fame may be underftood of that utter darknes *where fhalbe weeping & wayling and gnafhing of teeth*, Math. 8. 12. This feemes to be the moft abject, vildeft and remote of all the reft; There is the fame reafon of oppofites, *The Saints fhall fhine as the Sun in the glory of their Father*; And as the favour of God is called the light of his countenance, and the Saints are faid to be in light, fo the wicked and Divells to be caft into utter darkneffe.

Againe as the holy Angells and Saints are in the highft heavens, with God and Chrift, fo the Divell and reprobates, fhalbe in the moft remote place from all thefe furtheft from God and all good, and light, and comfort. *Between you and us there is a great gulfe*, Luk. 16. 26. This place may be either neere the Center of the earth, or in the depths of the great waters, that is, moft

remote

remote from the highſt heavens, and this appeares by that place Luk. 8. 31. Where the Diⁱells beſought Chriſt, that hee would not command them to goe into the depths, as apprehending that eternall judgement to which they were deſtin'd, and having it ever in their eye to aſtoniſh them, and dread them, therefore they were affraid of Chriſt, and beſought him not to torment them before their time; But for the preſent according to that in Peter, 2. Pet. 2. 4. *the Angells that ſinned are caſt downe into hell*, as wee tranſlate it, not intending by that the place of their ultimate puniſhment, for hee ſaies, *they are reſerved in chaines till the judgement of the laſt day*, as malefactours that indure a good piece of their puniſhment, by the hardnes of their priſons; but the place of their preſent abode is either in the aire, waters, or under the earth, as Eph. 2. 2. they are called *the Prince of the power of the aire*, and in that place of Math. *they beſought Chriſt they might poſſeſſe the ſwine*: And they carried them into the waters, the place of their abode: Some alſo live on the earth and under the earth, from whence they make their dreadfull apparitions, as hee that came up in the likeneſſe of Samuel.

Next wee come to conſider that place of Iude 6. I will not comment upon it, becauſe I bring it but as a proofe: The Apoſtle ſaith heere, *the Angells are reſerved in everlaſting chaines under darknes, untill the judgement of the great day*: By theſe chaines Divines underſtand, (beſides their guilt which bindes them over to puniſhment,) the divine power bridling and determining the Angelicall ſtrength, either intelectuall, or operative, ſo as they are not maſters of their abilityes, but are bound up and reſtrained, they have not liberty of acting, which the good Angells have, though God permit them to do much, and they are called everⁱ

H   laſting

lasting chaines, becaufe though by them they fhalbe referved to judgement, yet thefe chaines fhall fhackle and binde them for ever; By thefe words *under darknes*, is meant as before, the abfence of the light of Gods countenance, and alfo in darke obfcure places.

This diftinction of a double condition of the evill Angells till judgement, and after judgement, is neceffary to be knowne,(in refpect of the fubject in hand) becaufe if they were in their tearme already, and utmoft place,they would have nothing to doe with men, in regard of tempting, not with men of this world, becaufe they would be fecluded hence, nor with the damned, becaufe they in refpect of their condition, are already obftinated in ill, nor in all reafon do they punifh them in hell, for wee finde no peculier miniftery, which the Divell hath over them in hell, but they goe thither to be tormented with the Divell and his Angells, rather then by them, as wee finde nothing of the miniftery of the good Angells in heaven to us; therefore the knowledge of this is neceffary to us, that wee may know they are heere with us, not in their place and tearme, and that the Minifter about us, and are very active concerning us, which in utter darknes and everlafting fire they will have little leafure to doe.

Coroll. 1.

Let us confider this a little, that the whole univerfe of rationall creatures are under chaines and bonds in order to an eternall ftate, this will have an influence into our practice: Of the Angells wee have fpoke already,you fee how and where they are bound: Men alfo are in the fame condition, fome are under the bonds of election, others under the bonds of reprobation, referved both of them, by the chaines of Gods decree, to eternall glory or wrath, which is to follow; this in
the

the decree hath been for ever, but fince the fall the bonds have feazed upon men, and attatcht them af-foone as they have had a being, fo as they have lyen under the arreft clogged with fhackles, and chaines, which of themfelves they could never put of: They have had a wound in their wills, and a blindeneffe in their underftandings, the fpirit of bondage, through confcience of fin, and feare of wrath to come, have fallen upon all men, who have not gone fleeping to hell. Now then fee the ufe of Chrift, Luk. 4. 18. *Hee was fent to heale the broken hearted, to preach deliverance to the captives, recovering of fight to the blinde, and to fet at liberty them that are bruifed.* Heere is one that can knocke of your fhackles, can breake thofe bonds; indeed hee layes another yoake upon you, another chaine, by it you are referved alfo, but it is to everlafting joyes, it is to a crowne that fades not away, and it is a yoake, but it is a light one, not which fhackles and fetters, but advanceth your motion, and is a comely ornament to your necke, they are the bonds of a friend, it is fuch an imprifonment as excludes bondage, as gives liberty: Let thofe therefore that are invironed with thofe chaines, that are honoured with this yoake, glory in their bonds and walke as freemen, thefe are markes of their libertie, and badges to diftinguifh them from flaves; let them walke livelily and cheerefully, not as men bound up by a fpirit of bondage, and referved under darkneffe, but as men fet at liberty and in a joy-full light, with finging in their mouthes, and laughter in their faces, and joy in their hearts, that they may be knowne by their lookes to be the fonnes of the moft High, and heires of a free kingdome, and let your actions and fteps fpeake libertie, every one freedome from fin, from lufts, from corruptions, that there may be a glory in every motion , and an impreſſion of ſealing to eternall life.

2.   Secondly for thoſe that are yet under thoſe ill yoakes , let them conſider to get looſe , or they will finde a worſe ſtate behinde , they will finde themſelves, but reſerved to judgement, though one would thinke , the yoake they beare , the yoake of luſts bad enough , to be ſervants of ſin , and corruption , of luſt and pride , yet they are reſerved to worſe : Change your bonds therefore, reſt not till you finde your ſelves bound by other cords , bonds reſerving you to everlaſting joy and happines.

Wee have conſidered the Divells already , under two heads , one of their ſin , another of their puniſhment ; That of their ſin wee have diſpatch't with the corollaries drawne from it. In reſpect of their puniſhment wee conſidered them under a double conſideration, either that preſent, or that which remaines them heareafter, and founde it uſefull for our purpoſe.

Wee will conſider now of their ſpirituall puniſhment : Firſt for their will , they are ſo obſtinated in ill and in hatred againſt God , and Chriſt, that they cannot will to repent, and be ſaved ; They are that wicked one by way of eminency : What death is to us , that the fall was to the Angells put them into a pertinatious , and conſtant ſtate of ill, but the reaſon of this was the judgement of God upon their ſin , which was againſt the holy Ghoſt , becauſe willingly , and knowingly they oppoſed the truth and goſpell of God, therefore ſayes Iohn , *bee that committeth ſin is of the Divell , for the Divell ſinneth from the beginning* , 1. Ioh. 3. 8. Not hee hath ſinned , but doth ſin , that is pernitiouſly , and conſtantly, as a fruit of that great firſt ſin.

1.   For their knowledge that it is exceeding great in it ſelfe,

selfe, is without all queftion, they being of the fame
fubftance with the other Angells, indued with a moft
excellent knowledge of things, and a moft tenacious
memory. It appeares alfo, fecondly from their expe- | 2.
rience of things from the creation of the world to
this time. Thirdly from their office, which is to delude | 3.
and deceive the reprobates, and to try the Saintes
which require great ability of knowledge. Fourthly | 4.
from this that they are the great mafters of all the
impoftures that have bene in the world, of all *forcerers,*
witches, and foothfayers, who for title call the Divell
their mafter; Yet notwithftanding, their fin, hath
given their knowledge a mighty wound.

For firft their naturall knowledge is maymed ex- | 1.
ceedingly, there is darknes mixed with it, they loft
what man loft and more; Adam could call things by
their names according to their natures, but who can
do it now, and proportionably to their mote eminent
nature and fin, was the greatnes and eminency of their
loffe.

Secondly in their knowledge of things divine, and | 2.
revealed, in many things they fall fhort, they beleeve
enough to make them tremble, but many the beft and
moft things were loft to them, what they fee, they fee
but by halfe lights, and therefore though the Divells
underftood more of Chrift then men not enlightened
by God, and they could tell that Paul and his com-
panions were *the fervants of the moft high God,* alfo *Iefus*
they knew, and Paul they knew, Acts 19. 15. *they have*
whereof to beleeve and tremble, Iam.2. 19. they raife from
the effects fome darke and obfcure knowledge: Yet in
things of this kinde the *Divells beleeve* not very many
things, which they fhould have beleeved, if they had
ftood, and therefore are called *darkneffe, and the power*

of

of darkneſſe, becauſe they are exceeding darke in them-ſelves, in reſpect of the good Angells, and of what they might have beene.

3.   But now then thirdly to ſee things, as the good An-gells and holy people doe, (to wit) the beauty of holi-neſſe, the evill of ſin, the lovelineſſe of God in Chriſt, the glory of God, as Father to his elect, ſuch ſights as might gaine and winne them to God, they are per-fectly blinde in, and underſtand nothing of, (and as I have told you before, they never ſaw God as the elect Angells did, they never beheld the face of God;) ſo nor now can they ſee him, as the elect, both Angells and men doe, but heere lies the greateſt darkneſſe, which they can never overcome.

Their ſpirituall puniſhment will appeare alſo, by thoſe names, and titles, attributed to them in the Scripture, they are called *Perverſe ſpirits*, and *uncleane ſpirits*, from their quality and office, they are the au-thours of uncleane thoughts, and actions, they are called, *The evill one*, *the enemy*, viz. to God and man, *The Father of the wicked*, Iohn 8.44. Alſo *the Divell, the calumniator*, *the tempter*, one whoſe worke lyes in delu-ding and depraving man. Alſo *the God of this world*, hee would be worſhipped as God, as hee hath alſo a power over men, 2. Cor. 4. 4. So hee would have worſhip from them, as they have alſo formally, and explicitely from ſuch as perſonally give themſelves over to their ſervice. They are ſtiled alſo *the Gover-nours of this world*, or *Rulers*, 2. Eph. 2. which governe wicked men, in and to their luſts; Alſo *Roaring Lyons*, 1. Pet. 1. 8. from their fierceneſſe and malice: *A mur-derer*, Authour of our death and all murthers : Alſo *Beliall*, 2. Cor. 6. 15. *What agreement hath Chriſt with Beliall?* this ſignifies irregular, without yoake and diſ-cipline,

cipline, fuch hee is himfelf, will fubmit to no law, but what the power of God layes neceffarily upon him, and fuch hee renders his.

Coroll.

The ufe that I fhall make of all this to our felves, is, that wee dread the fpirituall punifhments of fin : Sin drawes along a dreadfull chaine after it, the little fweet that was in your mouth, that your rolled under your tongue, which you judged fo good, the taft of that is prefently gone, but there is a long bitter followes, the pleafure is but fkin deepe, reacheth but to your fence, but the effects of it are felt upon your confcience and minde, your moft noble parts; The pleafure gives you the enjoyment of a minute, fuch a one as it is, but the paine is of your life, perhaps of all eternity ; but how miferable is it to drawe on a trayne of fpirituall punifh-ments, that is, that fin fhall be punifhed with finne, the truth is, every firft fin, carries punifhment with it, for it is a punifhment to fin in the firft act, though wee confider it not, as all holy acts carry reward with them, even in their mouth ; but heere is not all, this fin fhall make you fin againe, *Pharoah* was punifhed by frogs, by haile, by many things, but the hardenings of his heart, as it was the greateft punifhment, fo it was virtually all the reft : That place Rom.1.28. is dreadfull, *Becaufe they delighted not to reteyne God in their knowleyde, God gave them over to a reprobate minde*, and then they were *filled with all unrighteoufnes*: If wee will not delight in God, God wil give us up to delight in the bafeft things in the world; Thou little thinkeft, that thy proud or uncleane thought, fhalbe waited on with fuch a trayne, not onely of punifhment, but fin.

And this is true to all in it's proportion, to the Saints, for fin doth not naturally difpofe for further degrees of finning of the fame kinde, for fo every act

strengthens

ſtrengthens the habit, but the ſpirit of God being
grieved withdrawes, and when yee are in the darke,
the ſpirit of darkneſſe is bold with you, and you want
light to repell him, and God can when hee pleaſeth in
conſideration of a ſin paſt, let either a ſin fall upon your
ſpirit, or an affliction or ſicknes upon your body. But
oh feare ſuch puniſhments, they are not onely of the
worſt kinde, but they are multiplying of evill infinitely, if God prevent not.

Beware therefore of ſin, leaſt you ſin, and leaſt you
be given over to a ſpirit of ſinning, which is the
greateſt and worſt of puniſhments, thinke that you
know not what ſins are in the wombe of this ſin, which
you are now about; If to grieve the ſpirit, to pleaſe
the Divell, to offend God, be dreadfull to you, feare
ſin above all, not onely for that preſent act, but for
thoſe other ſins which may be contained in the wombe
of that, and may in time be moſt curſed births of it.

And as Auſtin ſaid of hell, Lord ſaith hee, burne heere,
cut heere, puniſh heere; that is, in this life: So of ſin,
O wiſh rather the animadverſion, to fall upon your
bodies and eſtates, your outward man heere cut Lord,
ſpare my ſoule, my inner man, let ſinne rather cauſe
death then ſin, which is the worſt dying.

In the next place wee come to ſhew, what is the
principall miniſtery of the evill Angells, for God
knowes how to improove every creature, and not
onely the power, but the evill of the evill Angells, and
hee made nothing in vaine, *The wicked are for the day of*
wrath, muchleſſe ſuch mighty inſtruments and engines,
as thoſe ſpirits are, which though they have received
a wound and lye under chaines, yet are of mighty ability when God gives them leave to act it. That they are
at liberty for a miniſtery I told you before, when I
                                                    ſpake

spake of their punishment, for they are not in termino, they are not yet in the great deepe nor under the sentence of their punishment, they are not in the place prepared for the Divell and his Angells, but they are in the ayre and the world, where also they are Princes, they have the advantage of the place, and powers is also theirs; now for their ministery which still will come neerer our purpose, the principall and proper ministery of the evill Angells is to tempt, and induce men to sinne, they improove all the power and opportunity they have, chiefly to this, this is manifest by Scripture, assoone as the world began, hee began this worke with our parents in innocency, in the shape of a Serpent, Gen. 3. 1. Therefore Christ calls him *a murtherer from the beginning*, Ioh. 8. 44. For assoone as the world was, hee gave the greatest blow, that ever was given mankind, hee murthered our first parents, and in them all our posterity, and this was done in a way of tempting and alluring, so *Paul* 2. Cor. 11. 3. *I feare least as the Serpent seduced Eve*; shewing that that temptation was the beginning, the first of that kinde that was in the world, the first prancke hee playd, the first execution of his ministery, and as it were the coppy of the rest, therefore also Math. 4. 3. hee is called *The tempter*, as being the title of his office, other names hee hath which shew his power, and ability, his nature and his malice, but none declare his ministery so properly as this; Therefore 1. Thess. 3. 5. *Least by some meanes, the tempter have tempted you*, and very frequently our temptations are said to be from the Divell, so Ioh. 13. 2. *The Divell put into the heart of Iudas to betray Christ*, Iudas had the corruption in his heart before, which was fit matter to worke on, but it was a fruit of the Divells ministery, to suggest that temptation and put it into

I   his

his heart, fo *Chrift* told *Peter*, that *Sathan had defired to winnow him;* Wee fhould have faid hee was affraid to die, and being furpriz'd fecured himfelf by a lye, and fo fhould have imputed it to little more then the act of a timerous fpirit, but Chrift faid, the Divell was in it, and 1. Pet. 5. 8. it is faid, *hee goes about like a roaring Lyon, feeking whom hee may devour,* that is, by his temptations, and allurements, otherwife hee doth not rampe upon our bodyes, and Rev. 12. 9. it is faid, that *the great dragon was caft out, that old Serpent, called the Divell and Sathan, who deceiveth the whole world;* this is his worke, hee fayes, *they were caft out, and his Angells were caft out with him,* which are his under-minifters in deceiving the world, as Chrift Math. 25. 41. calls them *The Divell and his Angells.* (of the order of the Angells wee fpeake not now, but that there is a fubordination in their ftate and imployment appeares evidently:) But heere you fee the miniftery of the Divell, in the moft eminent branch of it, which is to tempt, to draw men into fnares, and to leade them to mifery: If you afke whence hee had his power, for all miniftery implyes a power from whence it is derived? I anfwer from God, *for there is no power but of God,* Rom. 13. 1. which is generally true of Angelicall power, afwell as humane, *thou couldft have no power at all except it were given thee from above,* faith Chrift to Pilate: Therefore this power, this confiderable miniftery to us, is from God, it muft needs be fo, becaufe els you would fet up another chiefe, another fupreame, from whence they muft derive it, and fo another God, every kingdome is under a greater kingdome, and what ever power there be, it falls under a greater, till you come to that which is the greateft and higheft, therefore the fame reafons that make the Divells creatures, make them alfo fubject, and

and if they be fubject, then the power and the mannaging of it is from God.

Now wee come to confider fome reafons, why God gives this miniftery to the Divells, why it is invefted in them by God.

Firft that the excellency and power of his grace might appeare, and be illuftrated, and what can doe it more then to fee the effect and efficacy of it in weake man, which yet through God is begirt with might, and made able to grapple with this mighty adverfary; So *Paul* when hee grappled with *Sathan*, and doubted of his ftrength, and therefore would faine have bene quit of fuch an adverfary, and fought God earneftly in the matter, had this anfwer, *Be content, my grace is fufficient for thee, my ftrength is made perfect in weakneffe*, 2.Cor.12. 9. which when Paul underftood, *hee gloried in his infirmities and diftreffes, that the power of Chrift might reft upon him.* They fay of fome fields that they are good for nothing, but to be the field of a battell; Paul had rather have his foule be the field of that battell, where Chrift fhould overcome, then be in the greateft reft, or beare any other fruit.

But if you object that the inefficatioufneffe of grace is afwell difcovered by this, becaufe even the Saints are fometimes overcome?   *Obj.*

Firft by that the Divell is no gainer, that little ground hee gets, tends but to his greater confufion, when hee is not able to make it good, but is beat from his ftrong holds, and forced to quit the field after a victory: As the Amalekites that robbed *David* at *Ziglag*, got nothing, for David recovered his fpoyle, and befides that, the other heards that they drove before thefe other cattle, and which hee called Davids fpoyle, 1.Sam.20.30. A man may be a victor in the   *Anf.*

battell

battell and not in the warre. The Saints at laſt ſpoyle the Divell, unthrone him, degrede him, as fruits of their revenge upon him.

2.   Secondly for God, his grace is magnified in ſome ſort by our falls, that is, it is ſhewen that it is grace, that it is freely given, and therefore when his aſſiſtance withdrawes, (as it runs not alwayes in an equall tenour) wee fall before every touch, not onely of the Divell, but of the meaneſt of his inſtruments.

3.   Thirdly it is Gods way, and it illuſtrates exceedingly his goodnes, and bounty, rather to bring greater goods out of evill, then to permit no evill at all, els no evill would befall his neither ſinne, nor affliction; ſo as Gods glory is ſtill illuſtrated, either by enabling us to ſtand, or at leaſt to gaine afterward, to the confuſion of Sathan, and his owne greater glory in the iſſue, ſo as the reaſon on Gods part ſtands good.

2.   But there is ſecondly a reaſon alſo of this miniſtery in reſpect of men, firſt for wicked men, and reprobates, God will have them hardened, hee will have them deceived, there is a worke to be done upon them that they may be ſurely damned; if you aſke the reaſon of this, *I will aſke what art thou ô man that diſputeſt againſt God;* and *if God will give men up to beleeve lyes and ſend them ſtrong deluſions,* as in 2. Theſſ. 2. 11. who is ſo fit to be the meſſenger as the father of lyes, who will doe it moſt hartily, and moſt efficaciouſly; and therefore 1. Kings 22. 22. one of thoſe ſpirits, preſented himſelf for that worke : *I will be a lying ſpirit (ſayes hee) in the mouth of all his Prophets.* So when God will have men *filled with all unrighteouſnes, fornication, wickednes,* as Rom. 1. 29. who is ſo fit to blowe thoſe bellowes, as the uncleane ſpirit, and ſince God ordinarily converſeth with men, not immediately but by Mediums and inſtruments,

ments, by men and Angells, by Minifters, and ordinances, who is fo fit for this bafe imployment, as the worft of creatures, the Divell.

But fecondly there is great reafon alfo for it, in regard of the Saints, of the glory and crowne which they fhall gaine by victory, *A man is not crowned except hee ftrive lawfully*, 2. Tim. 2. 5. Now how fhall hee ftrive if hee have not an adverfary, and if for a crowne, hee muft have a great adverfary in fome fort proportionable to the prize; Every Saint is a fouldier, as in the fame chapter of Tim. ver. 3. God hath put us into the lifts, he hath armed us, and given us mighty aydes, wee have a glorious king and Captaine *Iefus Chrift*, fellow fouldiers, the whole *Hoft of Angells* and Saints, and for prize *a Crowne of righteoufnes, a Crowne of glory*, therefore wee have a mighty enemy, whofe worke and miniftry, is to oppofe, affayle, and tempt, one fitted at all points for a combate, that knowes all the wiles in warre, and is mighty in ftrength, and the end is that great victories might have great glory through Iefus Chrift; but befides this, there are other reafons, as that this great enemy, this adverfary might drive us to God, and caufe us to fticke clofe to him; God would have us alwayes heere with him in a fpirituall converfe, as heareafter wee fhall be in a perfonall; Nothing will make us keepe our ftrength, as the affurance of a mighty enemye if you depart from God but a little, you are fure to be overcome. Now God that loves our company, hath formed this meanes, to drive us to him, and there to keepe us on fuch tearmes as wee may not dare to depart from him.

And thirdly that wee might be kept in an humble watching, praying, that is in a holy frame; What afflictions doe, that fhould temptations doe alfo, becaufe cause they are of an higher nature, and more considerable to us.

The Co-
rellaries
from
hence. 1.
First, that if there be such a ministery as tempting to sin and departing from God, let the Saintes blesse God for their ministery which is so much otherwise, that is, both the ministery they are for, which is to serve God, to doe good, to drawe men to God, to incite to holinesse (which is Angells worke,) and also the ministery they are under, for they are not under this evill ministery, as they are under God, and the good Angells, the wicked are so, they are in some sort subjected to it, for their good and advantage, but the ministery they properly fall under as their owne, is of another kinde, as wee have formerly shewne.

2.
Secondly then wonder not that evill men are so wicked, there is a ministery upon them for that purpose, *an evill spirit from the Lord is upon them, and God hath forsaken them;* be not scandalized at the evill of any that is not under the ministery of God, and the holy Angells, for they are prest and ridden by another spirit, and they cannot but goe when they are so driven.

3.
Thirdly, take heed yee be no occasion or temptation to sin, it is the Divells worke, doe not that vilde worke, it belongs to the Divell and his Angells; you may commit this sin amongst others, to be an occasion of others sins, though not of purpose, but through want of care and watchfulnes, but take heed of this, though it be but by accident.

4.
Fourthly when yee see men rise to a height in wickednes, doe not thinke they shall presently be destroyed, and sent to their place, they are cast perhaps under sure bonds, for destruction, but as the Divells, they are at liberty for service and ministry. God will use them as hee doth the Divells, for base and

and filthy worke, before hee will caſt them into the great deeps.

Fifthly labour for holineſſe and wiſedome, that yee may be fit for a miniſtry; The evill Angells are indued with great ſtrength, becauſe they have a mighty worke to doe, you have a miniſtry alſo, to ſerve God and man, to doe great workes, but where is your ability, labour alſo for holineſſe, that you may be mighty to worke. **5.**

Sixthly, if ſo good an account may be given of the Divells and their miniſtery, which is the worſt thing in the world, doubt not but God will juſtify well enough all his actions to the world one daye. **6.**

Seaventhly, dread not your adverſary, hee ſhall prove your Crowne. **7.**

Eightly, ſince there is ſuch a miniſtery to tempt and deceive, keepe cloſe to your ſtrength, depart not from your coulours, the Divell is to hard for you, if hee take you alone, ye cannot fight with him in ſingle combate, if you take your ſelves from Gods ordinances and wayes, you will be as an excommunicate perſon which is delivered up to Sathan, ſo you may deliver up your ſelves. **8.**

Ninthly, be ſecure on Gods ſide, this is but a miniſtery, hee will have the victory, and the glory, hee overcomes for the preſent often the infirme and weake will of man, but the power and grace of God never: Conſider that his power is from God, and his miniſtery is for him, in thoſe that periſh hee is the mighty miniſter of God, for their deſtruction; the ſkirmiſhes hee obtaines of the Saintes, hee ſhall have little cauſe to boaſt of at laſt, when hee ſhall ſee thoſe Saints, filling the ſeats of the wicked, and falne Angells, ſo as for Gods manifeſtative glory hee ſhall ſerve to advance it, aſwell **9.**

as

as all the other peece of the creation, for his effenciall it is above his reach, or that of any creature.

You have feene the miniftery of the evill Angells, it will not be amiffe in purfuite of it, to confider, how farre they mingle themfelves with temptations, and whether they be the caufe and Authour of all, or of all finne.

It feemes temptations goes before fin, as the caufe before the effect, Iam. 1. 14. 15. *Every one when hee is tempted is drawne away of his owne lufts, and luft when it hath conceived bringeth forth finne.* Therefore:

Firft to ftate aright the cafe of finne, and then confider how farre hee tempts.

How ever immediately or properly the Divell may concurre in the point of temptation, yet hee ever concurres remotely, in refpect of the fin committed, for betweene the temptation of the Divell, and fin, there ever mediates or goes betweene, cogitation or thought, in which the temptation properly and formally lyes, fo as hee may be an effectuall caufe of temptation but not of fin, for hee may neceffitate a man to feele a temptation, but not to confent to it. The Divell may reprefent fuch an object to us, but hee cannot conftraine us to be taken with it, to clofe with it: The Divell when hee temps us, hee doth not binde us, or altogether hinder the ufe of reafon, for though hee may have an ability naturally to do it, it is not ordinarily permitted him, or if it be permitted him, then properly and formally, hee doth not tempt to finne, but inflicts by Gods permiffion, fome evill of punifhment upon us, by which our power of finning, for the prefent is taken away, which cannot be without an ability of reafoning or working freely: To which wee may adde, that as the Divell cannot worke in our wills,

wills, the confent of fin, as being the next totall and
efficient caufe, (for that were to deftroy the liberty,
and life of the will, which is to be free and to moove
freely,) as hee cannot do this wholy, fo neither as a
partiall or halfe caufe to operating immediately with
our will, bending and mooving of it, for even this is a
branch of Gods prerogative, and exceeds the fpheare
of all created capacity; the will is independent upon all
created power, both in its operation and in its being,
and is out of the naturall power of all the Angells,
onely God the firft caufe of all things, can concurre
with the free acts of the will, and nevertheleffe preferve its liberty, hee can bend it, and frame it, and
reatch it, as free and as immateriall as it is.

Then firft *thy perdition is of thy felf, oh Ifraell*, it is thy
curfed will that ftrikes the ftroake for finne, which all
the Divells in hell could not doe; men will be impure,
they will be covetous, *they chufe to doe evill*, that is it
which ftrikes the ftroake, lay no more upon the Divell
then is his due, hee cannot force your will, and it is will
wherein your finne lyes, the leffe voluntary any thing
is, the leffe fin, nay hee cannot cooperate immediately
with your will, hee cannot bend nor moove it to affent
to the underftanding, the will and the deed is not from
him: Let every fin then humble us for the will that is
in it, and know that the ftrength of fin lyes in the will,
as that is gained, as that affents, more or leffe.

Secondly, bleffe God that hath preferved you this
liberty, and hath left to himfelf onely, that power over
you make good your liberty againft the Divell, and
call in God to your aide, befeech him that can, to bend
and moove you, and fince hee hath not fubjected you
neceffarily, do not you fubject your felves voluntarily.
Glory over the Divell in this behalfe, and make good

Coroll.
1.

2.

K   your

your ground, which all the power and art hee hath, can never gaine, unlesse you will.

For the second point, whether the Divell can con-curre to the temptation of all sin, some have thought, that there would have bene no sin, without the tempta-tion of the Divell, and that there can be none; but to make the Divell so necessarie to all temptations, as that they cannot be without him, I see no reason for though there were no temptation, from without, ori-ginall corruption were sufficient to raise temptations to provoke to ill, *Every one is tempted when hee is drawne aside of his owne concupiscence or lust, and intised,* Iam. 1. 14. So Math. 15. 19. *Out of the heart proceede evill thoughts, adulteries,* that is, it is a bubling spring, a fountaine for the worst streames: Also, considering how ready wee are to kindle and to receive fire from every sparke, without the Divell or any rationall tempter, sencible objects may betray us, *The lusts of the flesh the lusts of the eye, and the pride of life,* something of this nature is that which drownes worldly men in perdition, and destruction, and creats that conflict betweene the flesh and the spirit in the Saints, Gal. 5. 17. *The flesh lusteth against the spirit, and the spirit lusteth against the flesh, so that wee cannot doe the things that wee would;* by reason of this opposite streame, of this contrary power, wee are interrupted in our working; And be-sides, sencible objects which worke upon corruptions within us, which are apt to receive flame and burne, there are the ill counsells of wicked men, and wee may adde over and above, that without the foment of originall lust and without an extrinsecall tempter, man might have sinned even in the state of pure na-ture, why not aswell as the Angells, which had no tempter, nor Divell to fall upon them, which were in

their

their pure naturalls. And they which received so easily a temptation from without, as our first parents, might perhaps have sinned without it; Therefore without all question, if wee speake of the possible of what may be, men may sin without the temptation of the Divell: But now de facto, the Divell usually, hath a part in all temptations, hee findes matter in us, and hee workes upon it, therefore there are not many temptations, in which the Divell is alone, without us, and I should thinke there are fewer, in which wee are without the Divell. And therefore the Fathers were used to say, when you thinke or doe any evill thing, it is without all question, that yee have a malignant Angell exhorting you to it; Also when you speak idlely or doe any evill thing, it is the Divells counsell, but doe wee not finde the Scripture frequent in this? *The Divell put it into the heart of Iudas to betray Christ*, Ioh. 13. 2. So Acts 5. 3. *Why hath Sathan put it into thy heart to lye*. So Ioh. 8. 44. Christ blames them for being enemies to the truth, and for being lyars, but hee wonders not at it, for hee tells them the Divell is powerfull with them, and there is a confirmed relation betweene him and them, *yee are of your Father the Divell, and the lusts of your Father you will doe*, which may be said of other sinnes, aswell as of lying; so Christ said to *Peter*, *get thee behinde mee Sathan*: hee knew Sathan was in that carnall peece of policy, and so Paul speaking to married people, bids them *not be long asunder, but come together againe least Sathan tempt them for their incontinency.* What? Was there not flesh and blood in them, and corrupt affections enough, to make them incontinent? Yes. But they *wrestle not onely against flesh and blood*, as in the text, but *against principalities and powers*, against the Divell in all his strength and power, even in these

things,

things, wherein flesh and blood, assaile us also. So *Sathan provoked David to number the people*, 1. Chron. 21. 1. which wee would have thought to have proceeded from nothing more, then from the *pride of life*, and to have bene a branch of it, yet the Scripture layes it to the charge of Sathan; now besides these Scripture expressions this mingling and joyning in all temptations, may be supposed easily, in reason, by them which shall cōsider the innumerable numbers of the Divells, which are ministring spirits for that purpose, (as I told you before,) when yee shall also consider the infinite hatred they beare to God and man, which invites them with all diligence, and endeavour to fulfill this ministery, so as they have no intermission, no vacant time from this worke, the Divells Emissaries, (wicked men) how busye are they? *They can not sleepe except they cause some to sin*, they turne every stone, and leave no meanes unattempted, but the Divell himself needs no sleepe, nor rest, hee is not clog'd with a body, to weary him, hee hath no other imployment to distract him, no food or rayment to provide, to interrupt him, so as hee may minde his proper worke, and indulge to his proper lusts, which is to dishonour God, by abusing man, and therefore hee is ever at leasure either to offer temptations, and begin them which hee doth very often, or when any bubling is of our owne corruptions, or occasion off'red from without, hee is at hand and at leasure, hee hath heart and hand ready to joyne, to sharpen the temptation, and to give it those points it wants, to make it most taking; So as though possibly man may sin, without the immediate temptation of the Divell, as hath bene shewed, yet it is not improbable, that the Divell, out of the abundance of his malice, & solicitousnes to hurt, doth concurre actually,

ordi-

ordinarily, to all temptations, and so to all the sins
of men, and makes good the words of Peter, who sayes,
That our adversary the Divell goes about like a roaring Lyon,
seeking whom hee may devour: All this is that ye may know
which are the Divells parts, and which ours, and how
far hee can goe, and when hee stoppes, which is a proper part of this discours.

But if you aske and inquire now of the method, and   *Obj.*
whether usually have the start in raising and beginning
those temptations, our owne corruptions or the Divell?

There is nothing certaine, or assured in this, but   *Ans.*
there is ordinarily a variation, with Evah it was appa-
rant the Divell began, with Christ, it was necessary hee
should begin, and end, for there was nothing in him,
to fasten temptations upon; with Iudas also it is cleare
hee began, *the Divell put it into his heart,* and very ordinarily, according as hee is wise and diligent hee begins
with us, not onely in those temptations which men
say to be properly from the Divell, namely in things
suddaine, independent, and unnaturall, (which yet for
ought I know, may often have their birth in originall
corruption) but also hee begins in our most ordinary
and naturall lustings, and that either mediately, by
presenting the objects of lust, or passion, or by stirring
and mooving the humours of the body, that the body
may be more fittly disposed, to be mooved by the object, or els immediately, joyneing some internall per-
suasions, and reasonings to the motion of the object,
which may more easily leade and facilitate us, to the
consenting to such a lust or inordinary. It may also be
on the other side, that corruption mooving freely, and
of it self, the Divell may adjoyne himself, as hee will
neglect no probable occasion, to promote his worke,

and it is poſſible that ſome motions, may eſcape him
without his concurrence.

For though hee be wiſe and watchfull, yet neither
doth hee foreſee all future things, nor perhaps doth
hee conſider all preſent things, inſtantly, and aſſoone
as ever they are in act, eſpecially ſuch as give the leaſt
impreſſion upon the fancy or ſome of the ſences, which
may be ſuppoſed rather of more tranſcient acts, of
thought, of ſuddaine and paſſing things, then of any
thing of greater moment which lyes longer in thy
minde, and are premeditated, it is moſt probable the
Divell is never wanting to them. Thus you ſee how
hee ſtirres in ſin, and how hee mingles himſelf with
temptations, which is according to Scripture, and the
ſence and experience of our owne heart.

Coroll.   From that therefore which hath bene ſaid in the
1.   firſt part of the ſecond point (viz.) that our owne corruptions can furniſh us with temptations, though
there were no Divell; Let us be ſencible of the miſerable condition wee are in, and cry out of *the body of*
death, wee carry about us as Paul did, and learne to
keepe the avenues againſt all luſts, which may finde
away to us by our ſences, by the example of others and
by ill company aſwell as the Divell; watch our hearts,
out of the heart proceed evill thoughts, &c. The Divell could
hurt us no more then hee did Chriſt, if hee had no
more matter in us, ſubdue corruptions, mortifie luſts,
and the Divell wants ſo much footing, the fire is ours
alwayes though the flame be his, quench the fire, take
away the ſubject matter, and then yee defeate and
vexe him, as hee doth you with his wiles.

2.   But then ſecondly ſee the need of watching, *yee fight*
not againſt fleſh and blood, yee have a nature that you
cannot ſtand before without a ſpeciall aſſiſtance, that
                                                      yeeldes

yeeldes without a blow, or with an eafy touch, and wee have a Divell able to adde ftrength to the blunteft weapon, to ftir up corruption, where they are, moft mortified, *who is fufficient for thefe things* for this combate.

Fly to Chrift *to the Lyon of the tribe of Iudah*, to refift for you this *Roaring Lyon*.

Thirdly in our watching thinke much of the Divell, have him evermore in our eye, and by knowing his nature, wiles, and methods, and his miniftery what hee doth in the world, hee inftructed for him, as for an enemy, fet him up as a But to fhoote againft; But in our confeffions, charge onely our felves, Acts 5. 3. *Peter faid to Amanias, why hath Sathan filled thy heart*, hee chargeth him, reafons it out with him, not with the Divell, it was an evafion in Evah to excufe herfelf by the temptation of the Divell, and in Adam by Evah, therefore the charge of fin is ours, not the Divells.

Wee have laft infifted upon thefe two heads, what influence the Divell had upon fin, and then fecondly, what influence hee had upon temptations, and how hee ufually concurred in tempting, whether no temptations were without him, and how hee either begins, or joynes with us in them for the feverall manner or wayes of conveying his temptations to us, either by prefenting fencible objects, or by fpeaking to us, from without as the Divell did to Evah, and doth to many in apparitions, or by applying himfelf to our fancies, by an inward commotion of our humours, and ftirring of the phantafmes, thefe with the like it will not be needfull to repeate againe, but referre you to what I delivered, concerning the good Angells in the former part of this difcource.

But before wee finifh this head of their miniftery, there is one thing more which would be touch't: How those ministeries are distributed, and whether there be Divells appropriated to such vices or to such persons: Some have thought that some rankes or kindes of Divells, have bene to tempt, to pride, others to lust, others to covetousnes, &c, as being called in some places a lying spirit, in other a seducing spirit, in others a spirit of fornication, &c. But it seemes not necessary that these spirits should be ever divers, but that the same may doe severall things, in divers times, and may from the effects on the world gaine those names; nor is there any such distinction in the good Angells, but the Angell keepers, as you have heard before, promote to all good, oppose all evill; So the same Divell tempted Christ to many severall things, to distrust in God, and to worship him; So Iobs Divell had power, not onely over his cattle, and children, but his body also; And besides, all the evill Angells, have knowledge, power, and will enough, to tempt to all vices, and as much, as in them is, they will loose no opportunity, to vent their malice and hurt us, therefore others distinguish their ministery according to the object of it, Persons, and States, and Societies, and therefore quote these places of Dan. 8. 20. 21. where mention is made of the *Kings of Persia and Greecia*, which opposed *Michaël their Prince*, and understand also that place so, of 2. Cor. 12. 7. *There was given unto mee the messenger of Sathan to buffet mee*, and that curse, Psal. 109. 6. *Let Sathan stand at his right hand;* and the liberty the Divell obtained upon Iob, which are still supposed to be certaine peculiar Divells, set out by Sathan their Prince for that particular ministry, to such a person or state, though they must beg leave of God for the execution; This is not improbable, for Sathan hath ever bene the ape of God, and there is no doubt of his

will

will for this method, (which hee fees fo advantagious
for the Saints in the other miniftery, of which wee
have fpoken,) if his power faile him not; Now if hee
have inftruments enough and God permit it, there is
no doubt of his power, and where God permits him
to tempt, hee will fure permit him to ufe the beft methods, and of the other, (to wit,) that hee wants not
inftruments, there is as litle doubt; the hoft of heaven
was great, and there were Angells enough that fell, to
conflict with all men, Sathan could fpare a legion for
one man, to doe a great worke.

Confider the difference betweene the Saints, and
the wicked, in the point of temptation, I fhewed you
before that the Saints, and onely they, have good Angells for their Guardians, Heb.1.14. The Divell doth
not faile to allot them evill Angells alfo; But what
becomes of the wicked? *an evill fpirit is upon them, and
God is not with them*; this fhewes firft the excellent condition of the Saints, and the difference betweene them
and the reprobates; The Saints ly bound under the
decree of God, under the miniftery of Angells; the
wicked are expofed as a prey to the Divell already.

But fecondly let this difference in our ftate caufe a
difference in our working, and refifting, it fhould be
a fhame for the Saints to fall, and faile as doe the wicked, alas they have not thofe aides, thofe fights and
vifions, thofe contrary whifperings; where is the good
Angells that fhould conflict with the other, they want
the contrary principle, they want the externall helpes,
they have fome darke fights of God, fome whifperings
of confcience, though in great fins a louder fpeaking,
but they want the fpirit, the good Angells a new nature, therefore in thefe refpects, the fins of holy men,
are capable of greater aggravations then the wickeds

Coroll.
1.

2.

L   are,

are , and God is more diſpleaſed with them , they are not left to the wide world, they have *cuſtodes*, and *teſtes morum*, thoſe which are witneſſes of their manners and keepers , alſo , God is at the charge of giving them , tutors , and governours , great and holy guards , they muſt breake many cords, many bonds, before they can reatch a ſin ; Let this conſideration ſtrengthen us,and begirt us to holines , and incite us to pitty , and helpe wicked men , which that wee may doe the more , and may more fully fall under our governours , and tutors given us by God , and may ſee reaſon why wee ſhould not ſin as do others : Let us conſider a little out of the Scripture how exceedingly the wicked fall under the Divell beyond what the Saints doe, by the decree and permiſſion of God, Eph. 2. 2. *In them hee workes* (ſayes hee) that is *efficatiouſly*, hee workes his will in all the pieces of diſobedience. Alſo 2. Cor. 4. 3. 4. *Our goſpell is hid to them that are loſt* , *whoſe mindes the God of this world hath blinded.* So 2. Tim. 2. 26. they are ſaid to be *taken captive by him at his will;* hee hath them in a ſtring , hee can drive them to any madneſſe , or folly to oppoſe the truth, as in the preceding verſe, though it be clearer then the day, or any other thing. Therefore els where Sathan is called *The God of this world,* and the wicked, the children of the Divell, who fall under his lawes , eaſily and naturally as children doe , now none of theſe things is ſpoken of the Saints. Why ? becauſe they are under another God , another Tutor , other Guardians , hee hath neither that power nor thoſe meanes of deriving it,if Sathan ſtand at our right hand, our good Angell ſtands there alſo ; if the Divell uſe all his arts,God hath his methods alſo ; Therefore let it be no matter of our glory , that wee are not as the wicked are, but of our ſhame, that wee come neere

them

them in any meafure, and of our glorying and prayfe to God, who hath put us in the other predicament, where though you have the Divell who affaults us with all violence, yet hee prevailes not, becaufe you have God and the good Angells to oppofe him.

In the next place under this head of the Divells miniftery for temptation, wee may confider which way hee layes himfelf out towards mankinde (that is) toward the Saints, and others, for though his power be limitted towards fome more then others the temptations in refpect of the fubject matter of them, the things to which hee tempts are the very fame.

Hee will venture upon the Saints, even the greateft things, though perhaps in fome difference of method, that wee may fee by his temptations to Chrift, and the reafon is, becaufe hee is not ever affured, who is a Saint, and who is not, they may be of his owne; And becaufe a little ground gained of them, is a great victory, and becaufe if as fometimes hee doth hee can bring them very low, hee makes Trophyes, and glories in their blood and fhame very much.

To handle this at large were to make a treaty of temptations, (which I at all intend not in this fubject) for as I told you, there is fcarce any temptation, with which the Divell mingles not, but to point at fome heads onely which the Scripture mentions, or experience.

And firft, as greateft haters of God, and his glory the Divells oppofe with all their might the worfhip of the great God, and in order to this, they would hinder the knowledge of him, they would ecclipfe the light, with the greateft and thickeft darkneffe, how much they are in this, appeares in that bold tempting of Chrift, when the divell durft venture upon a motion

1

of worſhipping him, in plaine tearmes, and offered all for it: This all auntient and moderne ſtories witneſſe, the firſt thing the Divell makes out for amongſt his, is an alienation from God, and a ſhaped and formed worſhip to himſelf, for which purpoſe hee hath his aſſemblings, where hee appeares perſonally, as appeares by the confeſſion of many hundreds: And therefore Antichriſt his eldeſt ſonne, *whoſe coming is after the working of Sathan*, 2. Theſſ. 2. 9. (that is, who workes even as Sathan workes hee doth the like) ver. 4. *Hee oppoſeth and exalteth himſelf above God, ſo that hee as God, ſitteth in the temple of God, ſhewing himſelf that hee is God:* So as now to be of his party, is to be of Sathans party, to obey him, is to obey the Divell; let them conſider this who are bold to vary in doctrine or worſhip, from the word of God, they fall under a mighty temptation of the Divell, it is his moſt naturall temptation, they ſtrike at the root of all obedience, that ſtrike at the rule, which is the head of worſhip, this is to draw men cleerly and immediately from God, let us advance the glory of God; and the worſhip of God, ſo yee ſhall be fighters againſt Sathan, as the others are fighters againſt God, thinke the promoting of the knowledge of God; and the worſhip of God, to be the greateſt ſervice you can do to God, and the greateſt head you can make againſt the Divell.

2.   Secondly as I told you formerly, they are the greateſt enemies of Chriſt and the goſpell, which was in all likelihood the occaſions of their fall, *Hee ſhall bruiſe thy heele*, was propheſied of him of old, that is, hee can goe no higher, but what ever hee can, hee ſhall doe. Before Chriſt came hee oppoſed the beleeving of the Meſſiah, laboured in his inſtrument to deſtroy the whole nation of the Iewes, by *Antiochus;* when hee was borne

borne would have deftroyed him by *Herod*, Math. 2.
Fell fiercely upon him in the wildernefle , tooke him
at an advantage , carries himfelf , fo in every refpect
that Chrift calls him the enemy : *The enemy came and*
fowed tares, Math. 13. 39. And as at other times more
groffely , fo amongft the Saints more refinedly, hee
oppofeth gofpell-worfhip , gofpell-preaching , would
mingle fome things of worke and merit, with the free
doctrine of juftification , fome thing of doubt , and
flavifh feare , with the free glorying in our portion ,
with *joy unfpeakeable and glorious* , fome thing of pompe
or flavery with the free, and fimple governement, and
adminiftration of the worfhip,and difcipline of Chrift,
fo as pure and naked gofpell is little knowne , or
preached by the minifters and profeffours of it.

Therefore what the Divell abafeth , let us exalt , let   *Coroll.*
us defire to know nothing but *Iefus Chrift and him cru-*
cified ; Let Chrift in the Kingdome of Chrift *be all in*
all ; Let us beleeve, though wee be nothing, let us rejoyce,though wee be worfe then nothing in our felves,
that is , to make good the gofpell , that is, to refift the
Divell , let worfhip be adminiftred according to the
rule , though it want pompe and applaufe , and let the
power of the gofpell appeare in changing our natures,
in healing our lufts , *Grace came by Chrift ;* let the notion
of gratefulneffe worke in us , as effectually as that of
merit , let the love of God in Chrift *be ftrong as death* ,
let his dyeing love conftraine us to live to him , who
dyed for us, this is to magnifye the gofpell, which the
Divell would depreffe ; if you beleeve ftrongly , if
you rejoyce ftrongly , if you worke ftrongly , from
gofpell principles and notions , then ye deftroy the
Divell , then you oppofe Chrifts enemy ; I befeech
you , let us doe it under this head : *Doe I not hate them*

L 3   *that*

that hate thee, (faith David;) Chrift hath many enemies, which fhould be all hatefull to us , but hee hath none like the Divell (as I have fhewed you) therefore hee came to deftroy him: The faireft ground of contention that you will ever have with the Divell will be this, that hee is the mortall or rather the immortall enemy of Iefus Chrift, if you oppofe him under this notion, you will draw Chrift neereft you for affiftance , and fight a battell in the ftrength of love , and whilft you have your head, you will fecure the body and every member, this is to put another notion in to the conflict , not onely to fecure our felves from lufts, but to fave Chrift, therefore live according to pure gofpell , becaufe the Divell oppofeth it, wee have thought that to be affured or to rejoyce *with joy unfpeakeable and glorious* , were onely to doe good to our felves, that is the leaft in it , to a minde well-formed , the returnes are Chrifts , the glory is Chrifts , and the Divell (feeles every blowe) who is Chrifts enemy , and the enemy , God hath fet you up , with whom you ought to make good a warre and to contend for ever, as wee fhall fee heareafter.

3.   Thirdly , next to Chrift , and the naturall and Genuine doctrine of the gofpell, the Divell excercifeth this miniftery efpecially againft the Churches of Chrift , and the Minifters and teachers of them, (who are the guides , and lights,) and members alfo , either by perfecution or diffention ; How hath the Churches bene harrowed not onely of old by the Affirians, Caldeans , &c. But in the primitive times , by the Romaines, in all their perfecutions, and the Turkes ; now this the Scripture calls *the Divells cafting men into prifon,* Rev. 2. 10. All perfecutions, burnings, imprifonment, the Divells have done it , Kings and Princes hath but lent their hands ; That which the Divell did to *Iofhua,*
Zach.

Zach. 3. 1. *Stood at his right hand to resist him*, that the Divell doth generally to all those that would serve God in the ministry of the gospell: So *Paul: Wee would have come unto you*, (saith hee) *but Sathan hindred*, this their acts and Epistles shew how hee would have destroyed their ministry; Then hee corrupts teachers, *Sathan himself is transformed into an Angell of light*, 2. Cor. 11. 13. 14. 15. by whose meanes men give heed to the *doctrine of Divells*, 1. Tim. 4. 1. hee falls upon the membres also, pursues them *like a roaring Lyon*, 1. Pet. 5. 8. *Accusing them before God day and night*, Rev. 12. 10. First drawes them into sin the cause of Gods hatred, and then labours to fasten upon them the effects; this hee doth amongst men over whom hee raignes drawes them into murthers & witcheryes, and then discovers them, but his usuall care in the Church is, to divide and scatter, that hee may raigne alone, by difference of judgements, distracting affections: *God is love*, and love is the onely cement of communion; The Divell therefore, which is *the enemy*, with all his might breaks those walls, loosens this cement, that there may not one stone ly upon another till all be destroyed.

Let us therefore treade the contrary paths, learne the rule from the obliquity, aswell as the obliquity from the rule; It is warrant enough for us to resist what Sathan promotes.

In pursuite of that great peece of the Divells ministery which lyes in temptation, having shewed formerly what influence hee had upon sin, and what influence upon, and concurrence with temptations, wee came in the last place to shew, how those ministeryes were distributed according to vices, or persons, which when wee had made use of, wee came to discover to you some of the Divells marches, in his most ordinary and

high

high wayes, that is, the great and generall snares hee
leads men into such as seaſe upon moſt men eminently, and to their aſſured ruine, and with which the
Saints are ſo clogged as they are rendred unweildy,
leſſe expedite, and fit for ſervice, they drive ſlowly,
and oftentimes fall ſcandalouſly, though they riſe
againe: Wee will purſue two or three of thoſe points
more, and ſo conclude this head, in which I purpoſe
not to be large.

Another effectuall head of temptation, by which
the Divell labours to drowne men in perdition, is the
luſts of the fleſh. Peter admoniſheth to *abſtaine from
fleſhly luſts,* becauſe *they warre againſt the Soule;* The
Divell knowes it well, and therefore fights againſt that
parte, by thoſe weapons, *Our bodies are the Lords,* and
therefore wee ſhould ſerve him in *body as in ſpirit;* but
fleſhly luſts though they ſeems to be eſpecially in the
body, yet in truth they moove circularly, from the
ſoule to the ſoule, *Out of the heart comes fornications, &c.*
And when they have paſt the body and come to the
heart againe, the ſoule is rendred monſtrouſly adulte-
rous and uncleane, ſo that as the ſoule is pander to the
body, ſo on the other ſide the body is vexed and harrowed, beyond its naturall deſires, beyond what it
would have to ſatisfy an uncleane and filthy minde,
which appeares plainely in this, that the debordments
and exceſſes of no beaſts, are ſo great as thoſe of mankind, in bodily things, becauſe neither the reaſon of
bodily pleaſures, or any other conſideration, calls for
ſo much exceſſe, as the ſatisfaction of a ſoule, made
uncleane, and unpure doth, and therefore where ſuch
luſts raigne, and are in their exceſſes, a thouſand bodies
would not be ſufficient for the drudgery that a luſtfull
minde would put them to, ſuch luſts have no meane,
                                                    but

but not to be, such mindes besides other incōveniences labour extreamely under this unhappinesse, that they conflict continually with impossibilities, because their desires run still higher, and their lusts have enlarged them to a spheare, and capacity that no bodie nor bodily thing can reach or fill; How contrary this is to God and his holy Spirit, besides other things, two things shew, one is that hee pretends to be our spouse, and hath married us to himself in holines and righteousnes, sutable to which bond, and excellent alliance, there is a series of spirituall lustings; proportionable to the soule, the subject of them, and to God the object of them, which should leade both body and soule captive to an holy and intimate converse with so great and excellent a husband, whose comelynesse should alwayes be in our eye, and whose beauties should ever inflame our hearts, to whom wee should *be holy*, that is, separate, *both in body and spirit*, 1.Cor.7.34. whose loves draw out our affections strongly, but orderly, whose converse fills our minde and enlargeth it altogether, which is *health to our navell, and marrow to our bones*, quite contrary to the effects of other lustings, which give men occasion to mourne at last, *when their flesh and their body are consumed*, Prov.5.11. Now for this excellent spirit to be out-bid, by so base and harlotry love, that can make no satisfying returnes to have a spirit stollen from him, and layde under chaines, for these lustings are deepe pits, out of which onely an almighty spirit can rescue, to be cast of, as not faire or not worthy, cannot but be deepe in Gods heart. ------ *Manet altâ repostum judicium Paridis spretæque injuria forma.*

In a word to espouse the Divell his enemy by the mediation of filthy and base lustings, *it is no wonder that men are abhorred of the Lord*, when they thus fall, Prov.22.14.

Another thing that shewes how hatefull these lustings are to God, is that these fleshly lusts, in that branch properly called uncleannes, are made the greatest punishment of the greatest sinnes, Rom. 1. from ver. 21. to 28. If you aske mee how I intitle the Divell to this, besides what was said in the beginning of this head, (that the Divell who shoots at the soule, knowes those lusts ruine it, and therefore useth this great engine against it,) first how can you make a more proper match then betweene the uncleane spirit, and those lusts, which are properly stiled by God himself uncleanesse in the abstract, as being of all others most eminently uncleane and impure; besides looke upon men the Divell acts and posselseth most fully and immediately, *their God is their belly, they fulfill the desires of the flesh and of the minde*, which is ingaged as deepe as the body is in these lustings, and evill affections, 2. Eph. 2. 3. and not to prosecute this further, it is extreamely observable that where the Divell keeps open court, reignes personally, and absolutely, as hee doth amongst infinite numbers in this world, though wee are not acquainted with such assemblings, therein all beastly shapes and manners, hee doth subject them to the actuall commission, of what ever wee call uncleannes, although oftentimes greatly contrary to their wills and desires, that suffer such things from him, but the bond of their obedience is strickt, and they can refuse nothing, who have subjected their necks to that yoake, this, innumerable and joint confessions of witches and sorcerers, accord upon, of which I could give you account enough upon as good record as story can give us of any thing, although, which also wee may consider, the Divells are altogether uncapable of any pleasure, from such fleshly acts, who as being spirits, have

neither

neither flesh nor bones nor blood, they do it onely to debase mankinde, and by the most sensuall lusts *which fight against the soule*, to keepe them at the greatest distance, from spirituall, and heavenly employments, by which onely the humaine nature is perfected and improoved.

To conclude this besides what hath bene said already, the Scripture saith expresly, that not onely in generall amongst mankinde, but even in the Church, and therefore considerable to us all; It is *Sathan which tempts men for their incontinency*, 1. Cor. 7. 5. And it is from him that *the younger women waxe wanton against Christ, and turne after Sathan*, 1. Tim. 5. 11. 15. so as there is cause enough to entitle Sathan to this high way of perdition, to these *lusts of the flesh that fight against the soule*, and therefore cause enough for us to watch, him and our selves in this high way of perdition, in which every step wee take is a departing from Christ our spouse, to follow Sathan, for the Scripture calls it *a turning after Sathan;* Men are apt to thinke that it is but a turning after their loves, a turning after pleasures, but besides which you leave which is Christ your husband, you follow indeed Sathan in that disguise which should keepe us at the greatest distance, in every degree or steppe that way.

A fifth beaten path of the Divell is *Pride, the pride of life* you may know that to be the Divells way, from which God calls you of so earnestly and so effectually: first by his denouncements against the proud and pride, *Pride goeth before destruction*, Prov. 16. 18. as the herbenger or usher that makes way, a man acted and filled with pride, is upon the very brincke of the precipice of ruine, hee is dropping into destruction, God delights to *debase every one that is proud*, hee doth but stay, till they are proud enough, that they may be more capable of ruine, and deftruction, that they may fall deeper. Therefore *when pride cometh, then cometh fhame,* Prov. 11. 2. and they come both together, pride onely hath the upperhand; Will you fee how God fets himfelf againft this evill, Iob 26. 12. *By his underftanding hee fmiteth through the proud : Hee divideth the fea with his power,* as it is faid before, but imployes his wifedome and underftanding to fmite through proud men, that is, to do it moft affuredly, to doe it moft feafonably for their ruine; fo Prov. 16 5. *Every one that is proud in heart is an abomination to the Lord.* Nothing proud men, looke after more then to be had in efteeme, and in honour, to be admired, and to be to others the objects of their envies, and the meafure of their wifhes, the rule and modell of their actions, but faith hee, *Hee is an abomination to the Lord,* that men are which they are to God, and that they fhalbe within a while, to all the world, that is, they fhalbe a loathing and an abhorring, and therefore the things which they would eftablift fhalbe fcattered, & the houfes they would build fhalbe pulled downe, for fo fayes *Mary; Hee hath fcattered the proud in the imagination of their hearts,* Luk. 1. 51. that is, there is a concentration of thoughts, caftles that men build for themfelves, the imaginations, the thoughts of mens hearts drive to fome height, to fome high marke, or But, futable to the fountaine from whence they flow, a proud heart, and when they have wrought them up to a due height and proportion, and looke for the product or refult of all, then God comes as with a whirle-winde, and fcatters them, and fhewes how ill compacted every building is, how loofely it is layde, which is formed without him, fo for the other place which I hinted, the *Lord will deftroy the houfe of the proud,* as it is

Prov.

Prov. 15. 25. that is, not onely their workes in defigne as before, but their workes in iffue and effect; God may permit fome defignes to come to iffue, they may build houfes and get poffeffions, but they fhalbe deftroyed, it is a thing of no affurance like a building on the fand, either their foundations fhall faile them, or from heaven the Lord fhall thunder upon them, as Hanna fayes in her fong, 1. Sam. 2. 10. which is a proper way of deftroying, and pulling downe proud men, and things, which lift up their head to heaven, but faith hee in the fame verf. *Hee will eftablifh the border of the widdow*, that is, *a widdow which being defolate and afflicted trufts in God*; as it is elfewhere, widdowes who of all other lye expofed enough to injury, that have no great projects of their owne, no limits, or borders, but of Gods making, and little power to defend themfelves and theirs from affaults and ruine, God will eftablifh them, fayes hee, *the Lord will be their keeper, and then they need not feare*, there is no fence fo good, as what is of Gods making, hee hath bounded the fea by an invifible bound, his word, but no bounds are like it, fo if hee make a hedge about any, about his houfe and his wayes, nothing fhalbe able to touch him, and this leades mee to the other part, that bleffed part, which of all other graces is the foundation, the corner ftone to happines, and bleffednes, and that is humility, when God would bring his Sonne into the world, he brought him in the moft himble pofture; his condition, his fpirit, and his worke, were all of a lowe and humble edition, and whereas it may be faid, that this was for our fakes and part of his fufferings for fin, not fo onely, but efpecially and particularly, that, as of all other things, fo of this grace alfo hee might be to us the great inftance and patterne, and therefore himfelf fayes, *Learne of mee for*

I am meeke and lowly of heart, and yee shall finde rest, that which all the world seekes after but none finde, but such as are in that condition; so Phil. 2. 5. 6. *Let this minde be in you, which was also in Christ Iesus, who being in the forme of God, thought it not robbery to be equall with God, but made himself of no reputation, and tooke upon him the forme of a servant.* That is, whither ever his worke or condition leade him, into what ever abasement, into what ever lownesse, thither his minde easily carried him, therefore saith hee, *Let this minde be in you;* It may be you shall not be lead into such extremities, into such lownes, (for hee dranke deepe, yet the Saints are laid low often,) how ever let the minde be in you, have a ready minde, a minde prepared, there is nothing fits so for all kinds of worke and communion for doing and suffering, as such a minde, for want of which, either wee are not lead into opportunities of glorifying God, or wee loose them, and foyle them, and make nothing of them: Besides this (then which wee cannot frame a greater argument,) how is this frame commended to us by God, who best knowes what is best for us, and what best pleaseth him; Hee tells you *that hee giveth grace to the humble*, Iam. 4. 6. *That hee will dwell with the humble even as in heaven*, Isa. 57. 15. where hee will display his beames for comfort and joy, that hee may revive their spirit and make them live, the truth is, men are seldome empty enough for Gods filling, nor humble enough for his revivings, which is the reason why wee have no more of this heavenly influence, but are faine to spin our joyes out of our owne bowells, as the spider doth her webbe, and with contracted and bowed shoulders, to beare our burthens, which a little influence from God would make exceeding light, hee tells you all the ill hee sends, is but to humble you, and hee is

forced

forced to do it, *that hee may doe you good*, Deut. 8. 16. hee
tells you that if you will be pleafed with any of his
workes, with newes from heaven, you muft be humble.
The humble fhall fee this and be glad, Pfal. 69. 32. that is,
what God workes in the earth, if you be not humble,
you fhall not live, to fee it, or have eyes to fee it, *and the
humble fhall heare thereof and be glad*, Pfal. 34. 2. great
things are done and no notice taken of them, becaufe
men are not humble. The way to take in the comforts
and the joyes from the workes God doth, or the Saints
doe in the world, is to be humble, for proud men minde
themfelves to much, to confider God or others, not
to multiply more places, would you be great in any
refpect, Prov. 15. 33. *Before honour is humility*, and Prov.
22. 4. *By humility and the feare of the Lord, is riches and honour, and life:* If God have deftin'd you for thefe things,
that is the gate you muft enter at, would you be great
in the kingdome of heaven, take it in what capacity
you will, Math. 18. 4. *Whofover fhall humble himfelf as a
little childe, the fame is greateft in the Kingdome of heaven;*
But you will fay how comes the Divell into this charge,
firft as hee comes into all finnes efpecially fuch as are
great and crying, what ever drawes much from God,
or what ever God drawes from much, that is, of the
Divell, but fo is pride, as you have heard.

Another way by which wee fhall intitle the Divell
to this march of pride, is contention, Prov. 13. 10.
Onely by pride cometh contention, the meaning is, by pride
alone, that is, pride alone is fufficient of it felf without
any other reafon, to caufe the greateft contentions;
for inftance, men are not apt to fall into quarrells and
contentions, unleffe diftempered by drinke, or that
they have their paffions ftirred up by injury, or are
diftempered, or provoked, fome way or other, but pride
alone

alone makes men quarrelſome, and contentious to the
utmoſt, and therefore Pſal. 10. 2. *the wicked in his pride*
doth perſecute the poore; the poore middles not with him,
hurts him not, but hee is proud, that is enough, and
having advantage over him, being on the higher
ground, hee purſuis it. So what mighty reproaches
and revilings *Moab,* and *the children of Ammon* layd upon
the people of God, by which meanes they contended
with them, appeares Zeph. 2. 8. Now this, God gives
meerly to their pride, and therefore when in the 9.
verſe, hee threatens the cruelleſt deſolations to them,
he ads ver. 10. *this ſhall they have for their pride,* their pride
was enough to intitle them to all, that injury, and to
all that puniſhment. It was pride that cauſed contention amongſt the Apoſtles, their diſputations and
their ſtrife, *who ſhould be the greateſt,* Marc. 9. 34. that
pride was the diſeaſe, appeares *becauſe humility was the*
remedy, ver. 36. 37. Alſo Math. 18. 1. 2. 3. where Chriſt
tells them that except they be humble as little children, they ſhall neither be firſt nor ſecond, they ſhall
not goe to heaven at all, ver. 3. *Except yee become as litle*
children, yee ſhall not enter into the Kingdome of heaven; and
if there be any preeminency, pride obſtructs the way
to it; It is humility that opens the doore, ver. 4. *Who-*
ſo ever ſhall humble himſelf, as *a little childe,* the *ſame is the*
greateſt in the Kingdome of God; it is not hee that puts for
place ſhall have it, but hee that ſtayes till hee be called:
But it were well, if our contentions ended with others,
if that were the bounds of them, doe wee not contend
with our ſelves, our conditions, and with God every
day; Let a mans condition be never ſo good, never ſo
incompaſſed with mercies, pride alone raiſeth a contention, picks a quarrell, that is, that alone is ſufficient
to do it, if there were nothing els. Why are wee not
con-

contented, why are wee not well, when wee have enough, or to much, do you know what makes the contention, it is pride, *yee have food and rayment*, yee have not the leaſt part of mercies, yee have not the greateſt part of afflictions; what is the matter why doe yee contend, why doe you walke heavily and dejectedly, it is pride, pride onely, or pride alone can do it, can ſet you as fiercely upon your condition and upon God, as upon your brother, or your neighbour, yea when there is no cauſe at all; Its a glaſſe that extenuates goods, and multiplyes ills, and which is more then any glaſſe can do, findes them where they are not at all, this as I told you of luſt is a moſt boundleſſe thing, and will ſend you to impoſſibilities for ſatisfaction; for let no man thinke, it lyes in the power of his condition to make him happy, pride will outrunne it faſter then it can poſſibly flow in upon him, and which is more, pride multiplyes with the flowing in, as fire increaſeth by fewell; conſider therefore when you contend with your condition, when you are not ſatisfied with your eſtate, it might poſſibly have bene greater or larger, or fairer, or in a word otherwiſe, nay when you doe not walke cheerfully and thankfully and contentedly in what you have, (for that failing is of the ſame roote, and ſpring) then you contend with God, you murmure againſt God, and this a love from pride, properly and onely from pride, *for the judge of all the world cannot but doe juſtly*; God cannot hurt you, cannot injure, or provoke you, as another may, all your contentions with your conditions and ſo with God, are onely from pride; now I beſeech you who is the great Authour and fomenter of contention, but the Divell ΔιαβολⓄ, the calumniatour, one that breeds ill blood, that doth *calumniate and accuſe night and day*; hee doth

N   not

not onely accufe us to God, but God to us, hee accufed
God to Evah, hee told her *they fhould be as Gods, knowing*
good and evill, this temptation tooke, now hee inti-
mated that God made that reftraint out of envy, becaufe hee would have none fo great and fo happy as
himfelf, and therefore there was not fo much love in
giving you liberty to eate of the other trees, as there
was envy and ill will in reftrayning you from this, *For*
God knoweth, &c. And hee accufed Iob to God, *doth Iob*
ferve God for nought? A great part of his traynes are
fpent, in fowing diffentions, in making breaches, in
multiplying wrath where it is conceived, in boyling
it up to revenge, and then effecting it, and therefore
there is nothing, hee traines up his more in, then in
contentions, and wayes of revenging themfelves, to
the utmoft, the power of effecting which is ordinarily
the reward, his fworne vaffalls get for the flaving, and
alienation of their foules and bodies; to conclude, hee
is *the true king over all the children of pride*, Iob 41. 34. to
whom it may be faid as to Pilate concerning Chrift, *Be-*
hold your King: For pride was properly the Divells fin,
1. Tim. 3. 6. It is called *the condemnation of the Divell*, that
is, that for which the Divell is condemned; *Not a novice,*
leaft being lifted up with pride, hee fall into the condemnation
of the Divell. This therefore was his fin, and this he mul-
tiplyed and derived prefently hee faftened it upon
Adam, to wifh to be as God, *knowing good and evill*, and
although fome other finnes in refpect of the conftitution, and temper, may beare the title of the mafter
fin, that doth not hinder, but that in a true fence it
may be faide that pride is the mafter fin in all, it is
the utmoft roote in originall fin, that which lieth
deepeft in the ground, and can muft hardly be reached;
what are afflictions generally for, but *to hide pride from*
                                                    man,

man, nay, temptations are let out upon us, and some-times corruptions, that wee may not be lifted up, so it was to Paul, what ever his temptations were, the end of all was that hee might not be proud and lifted up with his revelations; this therefore is the proper sin of the Divell, and hath so great a root in us, of his laying in, at first, and of his fostering ever since, wee should watch him especially in, as that which hath all the evills in it, wee have formerly named, and is of all other things most opposite, and contrary to our peace and comfort.

Another martch of the Divells eminent in it self, and most dangerous and ensnaring to others, is that wee call worldlines, wee know the Divel is called *the God of this world*, and, *they that will be rich*, that is, they that set their hearts upon it, that propose this to them-selves, they will be rich, they will abound, they will, that is, what ever it cost them, though they breake never so many hedges for it, though they tread never so many unjust or weary steps, *they fall into temptation and a snare:* The Divell hath them in his snares, and leades them whither hee will, whither hee hath a minde to leade them, 1. Tim. 6. 9. Other sins have their ag-gravations, but this is the most earthly of all other, and in some respects, the most unworthy a man; And therefore the seate of this lust is ordinarily the basest spirits, there it hath its rise, and growth, and in order to effects, it is *the root of all evill*, that is, aswell as other vices, it is extreamely fertill of ill, whether you con-sider the evill of sin, or the evill of punishment for sin, this love of riches, what will it not constraine men to, they will breake all the commandements in a round for the satisfying of those lusts, what frauds, deceits, per-juryes, cruelties, murthers, hatreds have bene excer-

cised

cifed for the nourifhing of this luft, nay what other
fins of luft and uncleanneffe, of the loweft and bafeft
kinde? People often fubject their bodies and foules to
the fatisfying of this affection; And for the evill of
punifhment, the Apoftle faith heere, *that they pierce*
themfelves thorough with many forrowes, that is, they have
a carefull and forrowfull life of it, (contrary to that
good Solomon fpeakes of, *of rejoycing in their portion*,
and enjoying it with thankfgiving) they are full of
cares, and their injoying time comes never, for they
grow poore by their riches, they extenuate that in
their affection, which to their fence they abound in,
when they have more then their chefts or their barnes
can hold, their hearts tell them this is nothing : Befides they expofe themfelves to the greateft labours,
to the greateft wearineffe that is imaginable, they
toyle by day, and they cannot reft by night, the feare
of loofing pierceth as much as the paine of getting, and
there is no end of their travaile; But there be other forrowes alfo, terrors of confcience, and flafhings of hell,
which ordinarily accompany thofe luftings, and are
the reward and falary of their actions, befides the great
evill which I have not named, that *they erre from the*
faith, for having changed their God, and fet up *covetouf-*
nes, which is Idolatry, its no wonder if they fall from the
faith, and if not in profeffion, in deede, become a-
poftates; I have wondred why this fhould be faid of
covetoufnes, rather then of any other vice, that *is Ido-*
latrous, nor a covetous perfon, which is an Idolater, Eph. 5.5.
It is certain ambition, and pride and felf love is ido-
latrous alfo, it is true that covetous perfons worfhip
the fame things that Idolaters doe, filver and gold,
the Idole of the gentile are filver and gold, the worke of mens
hands; materially they worfhip the fame, therefore
                                                              faith

faith Chrift, *yee cannot ferve God and Mammon*, Math. 6. 24. Ye cannot put your truft in the Lord and in riches, the Lord and riches cannot be your ftrong tower together, perhaps it may be this, that though in refpect of our devotion and addreffes other things may be our God, that is, wee may ferve them, worke to them, labour to pleafe them, fo the Apoftle fayes, *their belly is their God*, yet in refpect of truft and confidence (which is much of the worfhip God hath from us) riches efpecially carry it away there, for the world hath got an opinion (though a very falfe one) that riches can doe all things, therefore they vale and bow to it, and truft in it, befides becaufe this is generally received, and *men are called wife, when they doe well to themfelves*; therefore the Apoftle brands this efpecially with that, which is a truth alfo of other luftings, that in a more intenfe and earneft purfuite of them, Idolatry is committed; Now in this the Divell as in other things juggles with us extreamely, one of the baites and fnares, with which hee holds thofe perfonally and profeffedly fubjected to him, is fome money they fhall get, fome hidden treafure, thefe poore captives hee abufeth infinitely, and after feverall yeares expectations of fome great riches, and many diggings and minings, wherein by breaking fome method, or other they faile a thoufand times, they meet at laft with winde in fteed of gold, with that which lookes like it, but prooves leaves or duft, when they ufe it. Remigius reports that of all the moneys, that the witches that fell under his examination, acknowledge to have received from the Divell, there were but three ftivers prooved currant, the reft were leaves, or fand, when it came to ufe; hee doth the fame in effect with all earthly men, either hee deludes their hopes, they get not what they expected,

N 3 hee

hee makes them labour for that hee knowes they ſhall
not obtaine , or deceives them in their enjoyments ,
they make nothing of what they poſſeſſe , and it is all
one , not to have and not to enjoye , in truth , that is
out of his power : The comfort of things, the good of
things hee cannot give if hee would , and hee would
not if hee could , the Divell incourageth us to cracke
the nut, but God takes away the kirnell, *gives it to them*
that are good , before him ; comfort and enjoyment and
delight are the portion of his people , *A mans life ſtands*
not in the abundance of the things that hee poſſeſſeth, that is ,
the good and happineſſe of life , and therefore , *A litle*
that a righteous man hath , is beter then the revenues of many
wicked , Eccleſ.2.26. *God giveth to a man good in his ſight,*
wiſedome and knowledge and joye, that is, *wiſedome* to purſue
right things , and to goe right wayes to attaine the end
hee deſires, *knowledge* how to improove them , and *joy ,*
that is , the good and comfort of things , and life ; *But*
to the ſinner hee giveth travell , hee giveth to gather and to
heape up that hee may give it to him that is good before him ;
they dig the mines , they plough the ground , but the
Saints enjoy, they reape and gather.

Coroll. 　　Therefore particularly to this , *let the rich man rejoyce*
in that hee is made low, and the brother of low degree, that hee
is exalted ; that is , ſhew them God , and heaven , con-
vert them,and they are eaven preſently,both are alike
neere God, and ſo comfort and happineſſe, that which
the world pretends to, but cannot give ; *Godlineſſe with*
contentment is great gaine , that is , which gives contentment , there is the gaine you looke after , there is the
happineſſe that wealth promiſeth , but it is God that
gives it ; now a *rich* and a *poore brother* are neere God
alike,if the *rich* at leaſt be made *low,*if hee have learned
not to truſt in uncertaine riches , if his pride that riches
　　　　　　　　　　　　　　　　　　　　　cauſeth

cauſeth be abated, and the poore brother be exalted, that is, that hee ſees not ſuch a difference in reſpect of ſolid comfort, and happineſſe, hee ſees himſelf in as good a poſture as rich men. Indeed that men are, that they are to God, and their true vallue is according to the proportion of their neerneſſe to him, not to what they are to riches, to Princes, or to the great things of this world.

So yee ſee theſe ſix heads wherein the Divells great temptation lyes, from whence wee have deducted ſome Corollaries, wee proceed to one or two more drawne in generall from that which hath bene ſaid.

And firſt yee ſee hence the drudgery of the Divell, Gods worke and the Divells, carries wages in their mouth in thoſe pathes wee have runne over, there is nothing but deceit and falſhood, a man is cozened, his nature is debaſed, and to judge a right, the reward of ſinning is not onely in another life, and in this life by afflictions, but the very ſinning is miſery enough, to be defiled and made filthy by luſt, to be puſt up and ſwollen by pride, to be made earthly and baſe by worldly mindedneſſe, to follow the Divell in all, how miſerable how vilde is it, how debaſing to mans nature? Let the children of the Divell, the peoples, the diſciples of the Divell glory in their portion, wee know it is their ſhame, they boaſt in their liberty, they have no tyes or bonds, but wee know that *to whom men obey, of the ſame they are brought in bondage;* now they obey the Divell, for they doe his workes, they fulfill his luſts; On the other ſide, let not us faile to glory in our condition, and to improove it, how ſweet is our portion, the traines the wayes of God are pleaſant, *all his wayes are pleaſant, and all his pathes proſperity,* to have naturall deſires, which exceed not their bound and liberty

Coroll.
1.

berty to fatisfy them, without the fire, the fcald, the
Itch of lufts, to have a fpirit fo great by meeknes, and
humility, as it is above thofe ills, it feemes moft to fall
under, to be be-lowe envye, for the world fees not your
riches, nor your greatnes, and above mifery and fhame,
to have a fpirit fo meekned as it cannot breake, againe
to be above your condition what ever it is, and to ufe
it, to poffeffe your eftate, and not to be poffeft by it,
to looke on money as a fervant of the loweft forme,
to pitty them that Idolyze it, and to improove more
your litle by enjoyment, then they doe their riches by
looking on it and Idolizing of it. Againe to goe further into the confideration of what wee faid before,
and fee how you outftrippe them for another life, in
knowing and loving that which they ignorantly perfe-
cute, in having your affurance in God, whereas they
have none at all, nor in any thing; I could be large
heere in the comparifon of our fervice and our way,
which fhould be the object of our joy and rejoycing,
when ever wee thinke of it, and thinke of it wee fhould
often, for that purpofe: For fince God hath made the
miferable condition of the wicked, a foyle to the love
of his elect, wee fhould do fo alfo, and run over by way
of comparifon, the heads and grounds of our comfort,
but I fhall rather in the fecond place

Coroll.   Intreat you to improove thefe things, *If you know*
2. *thefe things, happy are yee if yee doe them*; if you know
the differences of your conditions, if you know the
wayes of Sathan, from your owne, and where they
part, happy are you, if you tread thofe wayes and thofe
paths, and for thofe broade high wayes, thofe common
roades, thefe beaten pathes of Hell, which wee have
defcribed, our wifedome and our glory will be to keepe
a loofe of, to keepe farre from them, it will be leffe
fhame

shame for us to be shamed by other things, to be caught by other traines, then the common snares: Although it be true that in the pursuite of those things, Sathan useth his greatest wiles, and his finest peeces of subtilty, however let us keepe a loofe of, let us carry a watchfull eye to those great and common snares, the Divell may alter his method, but his *But*, and *end*, is the same, hee findes these things sutable to corrupt nature, and hee improoves all that is within us, to worke vilde and base impressions those wayes, therefore let us watch him, where hee watcheth us, and let us not thinke that because *wee have escaped the pollution of the world*, that therefore wee shall escape him, hee spinnes his web the finer for you : Which is the reason why I have spent sometime in these particulars of his most usuall martches, that yee might see the way in some of its foulnesse, together with the guide, that yee might see the hooke under the bayte, and be undeceived in things so greatly concerning you.

Now therefore having your adversary so fully and largely described to you, in his nature, in his power, in his ministry, as hath bene shewed at large in this tract of Angells,(for some peece of the Divells power, you must fetch from what hath bene said of the good Angells, that wee might not be obliged to repeate things twise) it remaines that wee should fight, that is, that wee should addresse our selves to the combate, for there is in this adversary what ever might prepare you, and stirre you up to a most formed and exact warre.

For first hee is as hath bene shewed a most inveterate and sworne enemy, hee ceaseth not to accuse day and night, hee knowes all our good, lyes in maintaining good tearmes with God; Therefore his care is to be-

O

get

get ill blood between us, hee inticeth us to offend him, and when hee hath done, hee aggravates this offence to the utmoſt capacitie of it, *Hee goes about like a roaring Lyon, hee goes about*; therefore hee is not idle, hee workes continually, and it is *like a roaring Lyon*, hee hath not onely a Lyoniſh nature in him apt to devour, and to fall upon the prey, but hee is ever roaring, that diſpoſition is alwayes wound up to the height, and intended in him, other enemies not ſo, ſo that heere is the worſt diſpoſition that can be imagined ever acted and mannaged, with the greateſt intenſeneſſe.

2.   But then ſecondly if his evill nature had not much power joyned to it, hee were leſſe conſiderable, leſſe formidable, though wee ſay there is none ſo weake, but hee hath power to doe hurt; But I beſeech you conſider, his power is fitted to his nature, if hee meane ill, hee is able to doe alſo much ill, there is no part or faculty of your ſoule or body, that hee cannot reach, and that at all times, in all conditions, in all poſtures, alone, or in company, idle, or imployed, ſleeping, or waking, when you are fit for nothing els, you are fit to receive his impreſſions; Nor is hee an enemy of the weaker ſort, and ſo leſſe conſiderable, an arme of fleſh, againſt poore fleſhly creatures is great, but hee is a ſpirit; Our originall ſin, our fleſhly corruptions wee finde evill enough, enemies bad enough, even to the making us cry out with *Paul of the body of death*. But *we wreſtle not againſt fleſh & blood*; this text tells you you have another kinde of combatant, for the deſcription of whoſe power to finde fit names, the higheſt compariſons will faile us, *Principalityes, powers, rulers, ſpirituall wickedneſſes above*: They are not called *Princes*, but *principalityes*, not *Potentes*, but *Poteſtates*, not *mighty*, but *powers*, Lord not of a part, but of the whole world, *of the darkneſſe of*

the

the world, all the wicked of the world , which are dark-neſſe are of their ſide, fight under them againſt us, and all the darknes in our owne harts is with them alſo, all thoſe fumes and foggs of luſts, all thoſe miſts of igno-rance, and unbeliefe are part of his armie ; Againe, in-ſtead of wicked ſpirits they are called *ſpirituall wicked-neſſes,* and that *above,* both in *high things* and *in high places,* they are above us , they hang over our heads conti-nually : You know what a diſadvantage it is to have your enemy get the Hill , the upperground , this they have naturally and alwayes.

Againe there are enough of them , they can imme-diately beleaguer a man, cõpaſſing him round, poſſeſſe every part of him : Seaven Divells can enter at once into one man , or if need be a whole legion ; doe wee beleeve theſe things, and are wee not ſtirred , are wee not affraid, if we apprehend the approach of an enemy, and the towne wherein wee are be in danger , what wringing of hands is there, what praying, what provi-ſion , and yet perhaps hee may be diverted , hee may accord ; But there is no truce in this warre , a perpe-tuall combate , that time you are not upon your watch you will be taken , for your enemy knowes it , if an enemy in warre knew certainely when the watch were neglected, hee would take that time , now hee knowes when you neglect your watch , when your faith and af-fections ſleepe, which of other enemies cannot be ſaid.

But then thirdly, if the contentions were for things of litle moment , the matter were leſſe , but if there be any thing great in heaven , or earth , that is the prize of this warre, whether it be the happineſſe of your life, the peace of your conſcience , the eternall condition of your ſoule, and body, or which is more, the glory of God, for all theſe are ſtrucke at continually.

3

Captaines when they make orations to their fouldiers, they tell them they fight for their country, for
their poffeffions, for their wives and children, for their
liberties, but what is all this to our warre? To our prize?
Wee fight for *peace of confcience which paffeth all under-*
ftanding, wee fight *for eternall life*, wee fight for *God* and
Chrift, whofe glory in us lyes at the ftake every day,
and fuffers, or is relieved by our fighting: I befeech
you are not thefe things worth contending for? Will
not fo goodly a prize put fpirits into you? Some have
done wonders while their lovers have lookt upon
them, others while they have fought for their loves;
What doe you fight, for nothing? Yes, it is a love you
fight for too, & one that fought for you even to death,
you doe but requite him, hee is before hand with you;
and doth not your love looke upon you alfo? Yes. If
you can fee him, I affure you hee fees you, and there is
not a watch you make, there is not a ftroake you ftrike,
but it pleafeth him, and it refrefheth him, as on the
other fide there is not a negligence, or a faile, but it
wounds him, and afflicts him; what fay you will all this
that hath bene faid put courage into you, and make
you fight, it is brought for that purpofe, I befeech you
let it put on ftrong refolutions to pleafe the Lord, to
refift this curfed enemy, this damned enemy, for fo hee
is, he carries his condemnation about him; and yet this
enemy which is left fo mighty, and powerfull, for our
tryall, for our reward, if wee fight manfully, if wee
fight the battailes of the Lord, (if wee be wife, if wee
will) all tend to the glory of our victory, to the honour
of our God; onely let us refift the Divell, being ftrong
in the faith, to which purpofe I will endeavour to fearch
a little into, and to fpeake fomething of this heavenly
armour which God hath given us for that purpofe.

Where-

Wherefore take unto you the whole armour of God, that yee may be able to withstand in the evill day, and having done all to stand, Eph.6.13. In this 13. ver. wee are bid *to take unto us the whole armour of God,* as in the 11. verse wee are bid *to put it on,* with the reason added, *that wee may be able to withstand in the evill day, and having done all to stand.*

From the first words observe this, that no weapons will serve to fight with the Divell but Gods, nothing will make you shot-free, but the armour of God, for so sayes the Apostle, *the weapons of our warfare are not carnall, but mighty through God,* 2.Cor.10.4. So as heere you see the reason, because carnall weapons are weake ones, to be carnall and to be weake are convertible termes, as to be spirituall, and to be mighty, are also; now you have to doe with a mighty enemy, as you have seene already, therefore you must have mighty weapons, you must have a wedge fit for the knot; David had never overcome Goliah, if hee had not come with spirituall weapons, 1. Sam.17.45. *Thou comest to mee with a sword, with a speare and with a shield, but I am come to thee in the name of the Lord of Hosts, the God of the armies of Israell, whom thou hast defyed:* It was not *the sling nor the stone* that did the feate, but it was this *mighty Lord of Hostes,* in whose name hee came; To goe armed therefore against the Divell in the strength of your owne resolutions, or your temper, or constitution, or your habits, and education, is to fight against Goliah with a stone and a sling, without the name of God; Nay your experiences, your contrary reasonings, they may have influence into your sin, but they will never into the victory, unlesse this stone and sling, these underweapons be mannaged by the name of God. For your resolutions this cunning tempter knowes that there is nothing so naturall, so proper to a man as man, as

O 3 change-

changeableneſſe, as on the contrary, it is the high and incommunicable Charracter of God to be without variation, or ſhaddow of changing, all the matter is but to finde a plauſible reaſon for the ſaving of his credit. For our temper and conſtitution, hee hath luſts peculiar for every temper. Beſides hee can eaſily perſwade luſts to give place to one another for a time, as pride to uncleanneſſe, &c. And his power is much upon the body, and the humours and conſtitutions of it, to ſtirre and worke upon thoſe humours, that by the helpe and mediation of the fancy ſhall worke to his end, and gaine the will and underſtanding : As for your education and habits, experience ſhowes that many things that looke like morall virtues, are nothing but the ignorance of ill, or the law of a conſtraint : Beſides hee hath his methods, and by a few degrees will leade you to that, and by ſteppes that would have utterly deferred you, had it bene repreſented to you, all at once, and for your reaſonings, and experiences you will finde that to be the proper weapon, hee is elder then Adam, hee is wiſer then Salomon, ſet holineſſe aſide, hee hath beene trayned up to ſophiſtry and deceit, and therefore verſe the 11. the *Armour of God* is applyed to *the wiles of the Divell*, ſo as you have no reliefe, but what was Davids, Pſal. 118. 10. *All nations compaſſed mee about, but in the name of the Lord will I deſtroy them, they compaſſed mee about, yea they compaſſed mee about*, there was a perfect *Pariſtheſis* of ill, and enemies a perfect beleaguering, ſo ver. 12. *They compaſſed mee about like bees;* you ſhall ſee how Bees in ſwarming time, will compaſſe a buſh, ſo will Divells and their effects multitudes of Diveliſh thoughts, and temptations; A man ſhall not ſee his way out, they are behinde him and before him, and as in the words following, *They are kindled as the fire of thornes,*

thornes , fo the Greeke and Chaldea reade it, they fall quickly into a great blaze, or the word is alfo quencht (as Hebrew words fignify often contraries,) they kindle quickly and like thornes, but they quench alfo as foone, *for in the name of the Lord will I deftroy them*, this is all your reliefe to deale with your enemies, as David did, *your faith is your victory, whereby you overcome the world*, 1.Iohn 5. 4. that is, *in Chrift*, it is *the power of his might that makes us ftrong;* Chrift hath a might, a mighty abi-litie, hee is endowed with power from above, which being put forth in us, gives us a power to be ftrong, and to ftand our ground, as ver.10. for in thofe words the habit feemes to be diftinguifh't from the energy and operation, when a man is acted by the Divell, either by an immediate poffeffion, or fome eminent ftrong way of lufting, that hee is ftrong in the Divell and in the power of his might, that is, you fhall finde a power full operation of the might of the Divell upon him, fo as did wee not fee a humane fhape, wee fhould thinke it were the Divell indeed, fo greatly is his might acted upon men, with power; Now after this manner fhould wee be ftrong in the Lord, by the influence of his fpi-rit, by the ftrength of his armour, other ftrengths will proove but weakneffe, fo much for that point.

Secondly it is not without its obfervation that it is called heere and before *the whole armour of God*, πανοπλίαν. There is no man pretends fo little to religion, but hee will doe a little, hee will pretend to fome graces, hee will make fome fallyes, as if hee would fight, but the difficulty, and the wifedome, and the ftrength lyes in the univerfality, there is a chaine in graces, you loofe all if you loofe one, as *Iames* faith, *Hee that breakes one command is guilty of all;* and God that gives you armes not to clog you, but to defend you, hath given you

nothing

nothing to much, it is not the beauty, but the use of an armed man which hee considers: That place which is open, to be sure the Divell will strike in; for hee knowes the bare places, and one open place will serve to kill you aswell as an hundred, therefore God hath made a defence for all, therefore the Scripture calls for *a growing up in all grace, or in all things*, Eph. 4. 15. 2. Pet. 1. 5. Therefore Peter calls for an addition of one grace to another till you be compleate. *Adde* (saith hee) *to your faith vertue, &c. For if these things be in you, and abound*, that is, if you have all those parts, and that in a way of height and eminency, if they be not scanty and narrow, then *you will abound also*, that is, *you will neither be barren, nor unfruitfull*: I beseech you consider this, it is the universality, it is *the whole armour of God*, that will alone serve our turnes, and which alone wee sticke at; All difficulty lyes in exactnesse, in bringing things to their end, and their perfection, every one is a beginner and a pretender to learning, to knowledge, to arts, to religion it self, but the exactnes, the universality is the portion but of a few, let us doe otherwise. How good is God, who hath given us a whole armour, let us not shew our selves at once enemyes to our selves, and unthankfull to him, unlesse wee feare neither God nor the Divell, on the other side let this comfort us, that there is *a whole armour*, there is *a whole Divell*, that nature is improoved to the utmost capacity of a rationall nature for ill, for hurt, if there were not *a whole armour*, wee were undone.

3.   Thirdly, wee are commanded to *take unto us* this whole armour of God, and ver. 11. *to put it on*, God makes it, God gives it, hee makes it efficacious, but there are our parts also, wee *must take it to us, and put it on*, there is a sluggishnesse in mens natures, if God would

would doe all, and men might fleepe the whileft, perhaps they would lye ftill, and let him truffe on their armour, but this is not the law wee live by, this is not the tearmes wee ftand in with God, what wee cannot doe, God will doe for us, but what wee can doe, that wee muft doe; Hee doth not worke with us, as wee worke with a hatchet, or a dead inftrument, but as the foule workes with the body, that is, in it, and by it, fo as the body doth its part, and feeles the labour, the foule at firft gives life to our body, fo doth God to our foules, when they *are dead in fins and trefpaffes hee quickens them;* Alfo the foule gives guidance to the body and direction, and affiftance, fo doth God, hee never failes us, hee is ftill by us, *at our right hands,* but wee have our parts, our reafon, and underftandings, our will and our affections, they come into play every day, and if God can do nothing by them, hee will do nothing without them; This, when men beleeve fo much in other things, as they will fcarce truft God with any thing, they will fee a reafon, and a meanes fufficient to produce every event, they will be at every end of every bufineffe, why doe they devolue all upon him in religion, without ftirring at all? Becaufe they minde it leffe, which is the meanes to make God minde it not at all; Therefore I befeech you, let us do our parts, fetch affiftance from God, and worke under him, receive influence and fpirit from him, and ufe them, intend mightily what wee doe, for it is to God, and for him; thofe that worke under any Agent, though never fo mighty, do fo, and this know, that the more mighty any fupreane Agent is, the more it intends, imployes, and fills the inftrument, as hee that ferves a wife man, though hee do nothing but by the direction and appoyntment of his mafter, yet hee fhall finde his under-

P   ftan-

ſtanding intended and imployed , for a wiſe direƈter
doth *more* intend, and fill the ſubordinate inſtruments,
and Agents not contra.

Now hee comes to the end and uſe of the *Armour* ,
*that they might be able to ſtand in the evill day , and having
done all to ſtand* , the word is ἀντιϛῆναι , *to reſiſt* , *to ſtand
againſt ;* you ſee heere is a reall combate , as your enemies are great which you have heard of before , ſo is
the combate , it will coſt you reſiſting , and fighting ,
and there is a day appointed for it , *an evill day* , that is,
a day of battaile, our whole life is ſo many evill dayes,
therefore ſayes the Apoſtle, *Redeeme your time becauſe the
dayes are evill* , Eph. 5. 16. that is , troubleſome and full
of temptations , if you would make any thing of your
lives , of the opportunities you meet with all , of the
occaſions that fall out, you muſt redeeme them, a little
time and opportunity is worth much, it will be loſt to
you if you redeeme it not ; So *all our dayes are evill* , as
Iacob ſaid , but ſome more eſpecially may be called by
way of eminency *the evill day*. All the dayes of Iob were
in a manner evill,becauſe none were without ſome mo-
leſtation , and trouble , *I had no reſt* (ſayes hee) *neither
was I in quiet yet trouble came* , Iob 3. 26. But the great
evill day was , when Sathan was let out upon him ; the
great evill day to the Diſciples was when Chriſt was
crucifyed, and they were *Winnowed by Sathan ;* So there
are more eſpeciall times and parts of our life , when
God will try us by letting out Sathan upon us , but
thoſe times and ſeaſons know no man , no more then
the day of judgement, and therefore wee muſt be ever
ready for them , upon our feet , and with our armour
about us ; ſtanding is a warlike poſture , a poſture of
watch,a poſture of fight, it is not a ſtanding ſtill,but it
is a fighting , a reſiſting , *yee have not reſiſted unto blood*
ſtriving

striving against fin; God expects that wee should *fight a good fight*, that wee should quit our selves like men, and wee had need doe so, unlesse wee would be undone, and foyled, and therefore hee addes *and having done all to stand*, that is, doe what you can, you will but stand, it will be little enough to doe the worke, the enemies are so mighty and great, the warre is so sharpe : God hath an purpose for many holy ends so ordered it, that you shall have worke enough of it ; some carry it thus, *omnibus confectis stare*, that is, all the afore said fell, and cruell enemies being overcome, having done all, having defeated them all, vanquished them all, you may stand as conquerour; What a glorious thing will this bee, that as Christ your captaine, shall stand last upon the earth, so you shall stand with him, glorying and tryumphing to see your enemies dead before you, when as others that were fainte and delicate, that would not stand and fight and arme : As they were heere led captives by Sathan, at his pleasure, so shall be led into tryumph by him at last : Thinke of this that by doing your duty, by standing your ground, by arming, and fighting in the power of Christ, in the armour of God, this mighty Hoast shall lye dead before you, *And those which you have seene to day*, in this evill day *yee shall see them againe no more for ever*, you have therefore two things to incourage you : First, the necessity of your fight. Secondly, the glory and pleasure of the victory ; Necessity will make Cowards fight: And therefore commanders provide dilligently, that their enemies may have a backe-doore to runne away, because necessity, and dispaire will produce wonders : I beseech you doe but see, and heere is an absolute necessitie, unlesse you take all this armour, *stand*, and *withstand* yee will not *stand* at last, this is little enough, you must doe all this that *having*

done

done all, *you may stand*, but then *having done all*, *you shall stand*, that is, *stand* as conquerour, *stand* as Chrift ftands, with your enemies flaine about you : You fhall have the pleafure of revenge, which heere you may take in by faith, and of victory, the fhouting of a conquerour; Cowards have but the pleafure of idleneffe, and the fhame and mifery of flavery, they *have their good times heere*, what is their good times? To fleepe, to be idle, to be abufed, and deceived, thy labours are better then his pleafures, then his enjoyments ; What then is thy good times ? *Thou art comforted, and hee is tormented*, thy captaine tells thee thou haft done well, *well done good and faithfull fervant*; Thy confcience tells thee thou *haft fought a good fight*, but praife is not enough in thy cap-taines mouth, *enter thou* (fayes hee) *into the joy of thy Lord*, hee fhewes thee *a crowne of righteoufnes*, which hee hath kept by him all the while, and which thou mayeft thinke on every day, till thou haft it, but then hee gives it thee, hee puts it on : Where is now your ambition, where is your fpirit, and your courage, thinke not on meane things, but on crownes, and victories, and glo-ries, and if you enter the lift, if you fight, do it to pur-pofe, labour fo to withftand, that at laft *you may stand; So runne* (faith the Apoftle) *that yee may obftaine*, 1. Cor. 9. 24. Every one is a pretender, and a runner, but few carry the prize, they finde hot worke, they grow weary, and quit the lift, *Thou therefore* (fayes Paul to Timothy) *indure hardnes as a good fouldier, of Iefus Chrift*, 2. Tim. 2. 3. that is, though thy armes preffe thee, and thy worke pinch thee, yet *indure*, it is worth the while, *that thou mayeft fhew thy felf a good fouldier of Chrift*, and mayeft pleafe him that hath chofen thee, thou muft not pleafe thy felf in his worke, *for hee pleafed not himfelf in thine*. *Chrift pleafed not himfelf*, this is written, God tooke notice

tice of it, the time will come when hee will pleafe thee, and then it followes ver. 5. *If any man fight , hee is not crowned , except hee ftrive lawfully or duely*, that is, it is not enough to enter the lift, and fight, but there is the law of combate, and the law of fight, if you do not fight as yee ought according to the law of combate, the law of armes, if you give over to foone, and ftay not till the victory be gotten, till your enemy be profligated, and abafed, hee had as good have done nothing, this hee amplifies ver. 6. by the fimilitude of a labourer , *The hufband man that laboureth firft, muft be partaker of the fruit ,* for fo *firft* hath reference to *labouring*, not *to fruit*, fruit and crownes , reaping and glory are the effects of labour, and due fighting ; thinke not to goe to heaven with your armes acroffe, or your head upon your elbow, or with good beginnings, and faint offers, t'is lawfull fighting, t'is hard labour, leades you to glory, and ver. 7. fayes hee : *Confider what I fay*, what were the matters fo hard, or the fimilitudes fo deepe? No , but the meaning is, turne it in your minde, often thinke of it, almoft continually, do not thinke to goe to heaven with eafe, you can never thinke to much that you muft fight hard, and contend lawfully , and labour mightily, and indure all things, as foldiers that would pleafe their captaine, before ever yee fhall be crowned and reape, and then hee concludes with , *The Lord give thee underftanding in all things*, which fhewes how hard it is, for us to apprehend thefe things aright , fo as to have them worke upon us, and to be affected with them to purpofe, fo as not to have fleight thoughts of them, though they be things not hard to be underftood.

To conclude, all good things are of God, though wee be taught, hee muft open our underftandings , as when wee are commanded, hee muft worke in us to

doe

doe, and especially in the things whereof wee speake.

It will not be improper heere by way of incouragement, to consider as what power and might Sathan hath, so what bonds and restraints also?

First, all the Divells can doe nothing without aformed commission from God, this the example of *Iob* makes most cleare, the Divell ruin'd his estate, by the Sabeans, but not till God had given him power, hee infected his body with miserable diseases, but hee was faine to aske new leave for it, so 1.Kings 22. An evill spirit offered his service to deceive *Ahab*, so an *evill spirit from the Lord* came upon *Saul*, but both by commission: So the Sorcerers of Egypt, they acknowledged the hand of God, when themselves were stopped, it was no more impossible for them to make *Lice* then other things, but God let them goe on a while, that his power might appeare the greater in giving the stoppe; So Zach. 3. *The Lord rebuke thee ô Sathan*, God can doe it though no other can, so *Christ* sayes, *The Prince of this world is cast out*, Ioh.12.31. *The Prince of this world is judged*, Ioh. 16. 11. hee is not onely under *God*, but under *Christ God-man*, hee is subjected to our friend and husband, and that in little things. They could doe nothing on swine without leave, Luk. 8. 32. much lesse can the Divell touch us in any thing, without a commission; Besides, what wee have told you of their chaines which *Peter* and *Iude* mentions, shewes the power God hath over them; And generally wee have this assurance, that *a haire from our head shall not perish without the will of our Father.* So as our greatest enemy is subject to our best friend, and mannaged to our advantage, which should incourage us to fight and secure us of the issue, *for the God of peace will tread Sathan under our feet*, at last, Rom.16. 20.

The

The Divell and wee are in earneſt, but God, as thoſe two captaines lets the young men play before him, and can ſtoppe them when hee will, hee is in no paine in reſpect of the combate or iſſue, but hee hath the pleaſure to ſee weake ſaints overcome gyants, by hanging on him by the ſtring of faith. God is on our ſide, and the Divell is ſo ſubject to him, as there is no greater ſubjection, let hope then aſwell as neceſſity incourage us to fight, wee have both thoſe arguments in their height; God will mannage his graces in us, to our advantage, but let us doe our parts.

Wee come now to the particular peeces of armour, whereof the firſt is, *The girdle of truth, having your loynes girt about with truth*, In the loynes is ſtrength, as is ſayd of *Behemoth, his ſtrength is in his loynes*, Iob 40. 16. In them alſo is the power of generation, for ſo God ſayes to *Iacob, Kings ſhall come out of thy loynes*, Gen. 35. 11. This metaphor therefore applied to the minde devotes ſtrength, ſteddineſſe and conſtancy; on the contrary men that are delicate, effeminate, and unſtable, the Latine calls them, *clumbs without loynes*, now that which fits this part, in ſome thing that begirts it, that the part wherein ſtrength lyes may feele ſtrength from without, and that is properly *a girdle*, therefore Peter ſayes, *Gird up the loynes of your minde*, 1. Pet. 1. 13. and Chriſt bids us, *Let your loynes be girded*, Luk. 12. 35. this whether men travell, or whether they fight, or both together, which is our condition, is neceſſary: For when they travailed, they uſed to gird themſelves, and the *Belt or girdle*, hath bene alwayes a peece of ſoldiers armour when they fought: You ſee now a reaſon why the loynes ſhould be girt to this warre: Wee need not goe farre for a girdle, the *Holy Ghoſt* tells us, it is *truth*, if you aſke mee what is *truth*, I anſwere in a word, *Right*

ſights

sights and judgements of things , and sincerity , this is that
which *girds up the loynes of your minde* , and therefore
Christ addes , *Let your loynes be girded , and your lights burning* , as before Luk. 12. Certainely cleare and right
sights of things with sincerity , are the most begirting
things in the world, this you may know , especially by
considering what is the cause of loosenes , and laxe-
nesse, and unsteddines in our course, and yow will finde
it, because men are either insincere and unfaithfull, or
misapprehensive , and darke ; *A double minded man is un-
stable in all his wayes* , because there is a mixture in the
principles of his motion , hee hath two objects in his
eye, two ends in his heart, and is carried up and downe
diversly , according to the predominant humour , and
quality, so as yee never know where to finde him , nor
can ever hold him, because hee is yours but in part, for
an end, such a one was *Saul* and *Iehu* , and so are all hy-
pocrites , the contrarye to which was *Nathaniel* , who
had this honour from Christs mouth, that hee was *a true
Israelite in whom was no guile* , Ioh. 1. 47. that is, hee was
a man round simple, candid, and plaine, which came to
Christ honestly, not for ends, for lounes, or to intrappe
him , as others did : Christ himself disdaines not
this commendation of whom it was said , 1. Pet. 2. 22.
that there was no guile found in his mouth , and *David* sayes,
Hee is a blessed man in whose spirit there is no guile , Psal. 32. 2.
that is , who is sincere in every thing , having his ends
what they should be , and his actions and expressions
sutable, that you may reade his heart in his professions
and actions ; such a disposition carries you right on ,
makes you steddy in your motion, without turning to
the right hand or to the left , *Girds you up* , and strengthens your minde to motions, to fightings, makes you
intend what you doe strongly , because you doe but
one

one thing, that which put *Martha*, into such a distemper was, *because shee was troubled about many things*, you see then, now how sincerity begirts, & how in sincerity & double mindednesse loosens your loynes, & nerves, but doth not misjudging and darknes doe the same, loosen your loynes, making you unsteddy, and weake, contrary to this begirting? You will finde it doth: Men are what they see, and what they judge, and no other, and though some men doe not fill up their light, yet none goe beyond it, a man wants courage that wants light, and *Hee that walkes in darknesse knowes not whither hee goes*, and that is contrary to this begirting, and hee must needs make many false paces, for hee knowes not whither hee goes, *If a man walke in the night hee stumbleth, because there is no light in him*, Ioh. 11. 10. *In him-* hee hath the instrument of seeing, the eye, but there is no light shining upon that eye, though a man should be sincere, if hee want right lights and sights of things hee will be rendered the weaker and more unsteddy, hee will stumble often, with a good intention about him, nothing gives more courage then knowledge, nothing intimidates more then ignorance; Againe, comfort and joy renders strong and steddy, now light is the embleme of joy, and therefore when the Angell came to poore Peter, fettred in chaines, as hee was, *a light shined in the prison*, Acts 12. 7. so sayes David, *The Lord is my light and my salvation, whom shall I feare*, Psf. 27. 1. and when in a low condition hee expected comfort from God, *Thou wilt save the afflicted people*, sayes hee, *but wilt bring downe high lookes; for thou wilt light my candle* (sayes hee) *the Lord will en lighten my darkenesse*, Psal. 13. 27. 28. Now comfort begirts, & comfort you see comes in by light: Againe. Glory, the apprehension of it, the notion of it, begirts, & renders strong exceedingly, *Christ, for the glory set before him,*

him, &c. did wonders, but light and glory runne together, and the notion of glory comes in by light, Ifa.
60. 1. 2. *Arife, fhine, for thy light is come, and the glory of
the Lord is rifen upon thee*, fo it is called, *The light of the
glorious goſpell*, 2. Cor. 4. 4. there would have bene no
glory feene if there had bene no light, and there is a
glory alfo in light, Acts 22. 11. Paul faid, hee could not
fee, *for the glory of the light*, therefore light is glorious,
now this dazelled his bodily eyes, but our ſpirits fee
better and more ftrongly for glorious lights, which
gives affurance, and courage, and fo ftrength alfo; In
a word, our whole armour is called *the armour of light*,
Rom. 13. 12. So great a thing is light to armour and
to ftrength, according to the more or leffe, of which
men are weake or ftrong to any courfe to which they
pretend, but above all to religion: Now for the Divell
againft whom wee arme, doth not hee play in the
darke almoft altogether, when hee would deceive our
fence, hee cafts fand in our eyes, mifts before us, to
deceive and blinde us, and then wee judge of things
not as they are, but according to the medium wee fee
through: So for our comfort how doth hee enervate
us, and loofen our loynes, by leading us into darke
thoughts of God, and of our condition, how doth hee
unfteddy our fteps, and intimidate us, by putting
fcruples in our wayes, and hiding from us thofe truths,
wherein our ftrength would confift; If hee can make
us infincere, hee hath enough, wee fhall then feeke
darknes, and chufe it rather then light, of fuch Chrift
fayes, that *they loved darknes rather then light, becauſe their
deeds were evill*, Ioh. 3. 19. But be fincere, the right
eyeing, the right feeing, the right apprehenfion of
things is that truth which begirts us, and together
with fincerity renders us ftrong and mighty to fight
with

with him, to conteſt with his wiles, with his lyes, with
his impoſtures, for his dealings with us is nothing els :
But be wee but ſincere, that is, honeſt to your ſelves
and to God, and diſcover him, and hee is gone ; This
therefore is a neate cleane peece of armour, fitted for
the part, and for the enemy wee conteſt with all. If you
aſke what you ſhall doe for it, I would adviſe you by
way of corrolary to two things,

Firſt, converſe much with the Father of lights, *In his*
light wee ſhall ſee light, Pſal. 36.9. Be neere God that hee *Corroll.*
may ſhine upon you continually, hee hath no falſe
lights as impoſtures have to ſhew their wares by, what
ever light hee affords you, is right, and gives you the
thing as it is ; Hee hath no falſe glaſſes, that greaten,
or leſſen the proportion of things, but ſuch as render
them as they are. Converſe much with the word the
booke of lights, all it ſayes is true without a reaſon,
though it be all reaſon, converſe with the Saints the
ſubjects of lights, they have light that will ſhine before
you, all theſe lights convey truth to you, the right notion of things ; And that is it which begirts you, renders you ſtrong and ſteddy, fit to deale with the Divell, the father of all impoſtures and deceits, alſo
think, ruminate much of things according to what
true notion you have ever had of them ; in ſome times
and parts of our lives wee have right notions of things,
with ſuch ſight as carry their owne evidence with
them, repreſent them often to your ſelves, this will
make your light ſhine to you, your light may be under
a buſhell in your owne heart, and truth without this,
may be to ſeeke when you ſhould uſe it, when you
ſhould judge and walke by it, you may have many right
principles in you, but Raked under Aſhes, but wiſedome
is to have them at hand and for uſe, that when the Di-

vell

vell comes with his wiles and his mifts, fhining and
blazing, truth may fcatter them and melt them, and
caufe them to wafte away affoone as they dare to appeare. for example. If hee fhall fhew the pompe and
glittering of titles and honour, and would lead you out
of your way, by that foolifh fhine; a right judgement of
things hath for him, that the outfides of things are
for children, that the mafks and vizards, either of
good or ill are not much confiderable, that honour is
in truth, that which is lafting, which hath its rife in
worth, and is given by God, and wife men, that fuch
honour properly fhould rather follow, then lead good
actions, that the praife of men and the praife of God
are feldome confiftent, that it is a figne of diffidence
of God, to be too anxious to receive honour from men,
that there is no reafon *that* fhould moove you, which
the Divell can neither give, nor continue to you: I
give you but a taft, if hee tempt you to gratify the flefh
by luft or idleneffe, by a foft and delicate life, by in-
dulgeing to bodily things, *Truth* will *girde your loynes*,
and make you ftand fteddy heere in alfo, by telling him
that it is wifedome to till the better part, that nothing
ftands in fo proper an antipathy to the fpirit as the
flefh, that *Paul beat downe his body and brought it into fub-
jection*, that the body is to be confidered onely as an inftrument and not to be idolized and indulged to, for
it felfe, that belly & meat fhall both be deftroyed ere
long, but the foule dies not, that idlenes is death before your time, with this difference, that it is confiderable in your punifhment, which death properly is not,
for no man is punifhed for dying; That Iefus Chrift
was a perpetuall motion, that good men have ufed to
finde little reft but in their confciences, and their
graves, till they come to heaven, that your condition
                                                      heere

heere is to *be a souldier, to indure hardnes, and fight,* for which truth armes you, not to live delicately and take your ease, this might be enlarged in many other particulars, and in these more fully, I onely give an instance, that you may know what I would, and may learne to begirt your selves with right notions, against the wiles of the Divell.

For the other part, namely sincerity, for the heightening and improoving of that, I shall put upon you but this burthen, *love much;* sincerity is immixednesse, and rightnesse of ends, a spirit goeing right forward, drawne right forth, without guile or ends; Love will concentrate all in God, make all lines meet in him, self love makes men insincere to God and others, because it drawes away from the pretensions which are to God, it sucks away the sappe and the juice that should goe into the body of the tree, it is like a cut that draynes the channell, which should runne with full source into the sea; but love gives all and wishes for more, in no respect so much as to give that also, so as it gathers up the soule and girds up the loynes for God, as bring what subtilties and wiles you will, it measures, all you say by Gods interest, so as offer as before, honours, or pleasures, or lusts, it will aske you; what is this to God, how doth it suite with his ends, how doth it comply with his glory, how is it squared to his liking and good pleasure, since you live if hee be pleased, you are happy if hee be glorifyed, love hath made you so much his, that nothing can be good to you but what is to him, love hath given all in grosse, and therefore can reteyne nothing in retayle, that therefore to mix your actions or your ends, is to divide you from God, who is your love, and under a coulour of bettering your condition to rob God, and

Q 3   undoe

undoe your self together, for love is wife, and will tell
you alſo, that it is good looſing your ſelf in God, and
that when by ſtudying for God, you forget your ſelves,
you are then moſt of all remembred ; I ſhall adde no
more, ſo much for this firſt peece, onely remember
to act theſe notions, and ſincerity in the vertue and
power of him, who is the reall and eſſentiall *truth Ieſus
Chriſt.*

You have already heard of that peece, which gives
the great and generall impreſſe, that which ſtrengthens
the part of ſtrength, that which renders fit and prepared for every good thing, and which is of exceeding
great influence into this battaile, *The girdle of truth,*
that is ſuch fights, and ſuch a diſpoſition of ſpirit as
begirts and ſtrengthens to what wee ſhould doe. Wee
come now to arme the breaſt which lyes as much expoſed, and is as conſiderable as any part ; For the breaſt
containes the noble and vitall parts, the heart, the
lungs, the liver, and for this there is a *Plate, a breaſt-plate,*
and that is *righteouſneſſe,* this Chriſt our captaine put on
before us, If. 59. 17. *Hee put on righteouſnes as a breaſt-plate,*
and wee, according to the duty of a ſouldier that takes
his example from the captaine, for ſo ſay your brave
commanders (whether in order to fighting or armeing)
what you ſee mee doe, doe yee likewiſe, and according
to the charracter and impreſſion which wee receive
from his fulneſſe, wee take on *righteouſnes* alſo as a *breaſt-*
plate ; if you aſke mee what this peece is, for it muſt
be ſomething ſpirituall, by which you deale with the
Divell, I anſwere that it is holyneſſe, and innocency
of life ; The firſt peece was ſincerity or integrety (as
it lay in the will) reſpecting the end and ayme of all
our actions, which having a continuall and direct influence upon the end begirts exceedingly; This is the
walke

walke of a Christian in order to that end, that righteous and holy frame of spirit by which hee walkes and mooves, *justly and holily* in all his actions, this is that wherein Paul excercised himself so much, *to have a conscience voyd of offence, towards God and man*, Acts 24. 16. That is, so to walke as neither to offend the conscience of another, by any scandall or stumbling blocke, nor to offend or wound his owne; This if you take it generally, one may call perhaps sanctification, not taking sanctification as it is, some times for consecration or seperation, as the vessells or dayes were consecrated, or set a part, but for sanctity, that is, inherent righteousnes, or holynes, or more particularly considering it in the walks and motions of it, it may be distinguish't into *Piety* or *Godlinesse*, and *Iustice* or *righteousnes*, the one respecting God more immediately, the other men; Such a distinction you have, Rom. 1. 18. *The wrath of God is revealed from heaven, against all ungodlinesse and unrighteousnes of men*, so Titus 2. 12. *Wee are to live soberly, righteously and godly*, there is the distinction of *righteousnes and godlinesse*, to which *sobriety* or *temperance* is added, as a meanes of doing it, and living so, because by it wee deny our selves in wordly lusts, as the words before are, *denying ungodlinesse and worldly lusts*, upon these two feete therefore, *this sanctity or righteousnes* mooves vizt. Religion towards God, and Iustice towards men: To pursue these tracts, were to give you the whole walke of religion, which is not my intent, for I give you now, but an exposition in order to our combate, onely a few things: In this righteousnes there is an order, *they gave themselves first to the Lord, and after to us, by the will of God*, 2. Cor. 8. 5. God must be first considered, and secondly, what ever you doe to men, it must be for God, and *as to the Lord, and not to men*, that is, not making them the

Alpha

Alpha or *Omega* the rife , or the ultimate end of any of
our motions, fo as motions to wards God, are firft and
efpecially to be confidered, *Firft feeke the Kingdome of God,*
& David fayes often, *early in the morning will I feeke thee,*
ftill God is efpecially to be confidered, *Hee that loves fa-*
ther or mother more then mee, is not worthy of mee, Mat. 10. 37.
and therefore in refpeᴄt of intenceneffe, you muft *Love*
God with all your hart , and foule , and minde, & though wee
are to doe aᴄts of righteoufnes to wards our brethren ,
with all our ftrength, yet that intenceneffe is required
efpecially in refpeᴄt of God , and by the vertue of religion ; As for righteoufneffe towards man , it is that
by which wee are inclined, to give every one that duty
and obfervance which is their due, and under this confideration, falls all men, with whom wee have to doe ,
and Angells alfo , for fince God onely is the objeᴄt of
religious worfhip, they muft fall under the notion and
confideration of *our brethren or neighbours,* for in refufing
worfhip, they fay, *they are our fellow-fervants, & of our bre-*
thren the Prophets, and of them which keepe the fayings of the
booke of God; fo as they refufe not their due, but Gods
due, which is religious worfhip, Rev. 22. 9. and of that
moment is this righteoufnes , towards our brother ;
that the truth of religion towards God, cannot confift
with the negleᴄt of this , if a man *fay hee loves God, and*
hates his brother, hee is a lyar , 1. Ioh. 4. 20. *And this com-*
mandement have wee of God , that hee that loves God fhould
love his brother alfo : This in the negative is a fure argument , that there is no religion towards God, where
there is not righteoufnes towards men, Gall. 5. 19. *The*
workes of the flefh are manifeft (faith Paul,) unrighteous,
unworthy aᴄtions , clearily manifeft a wicked man, if
hee be unrighteous and unjuft towards men , hee is
irreligious towards God.

                                                    This

This righteoufnes hath for its meafure, or rule, the love wee beare our felves, for God being loved by us, with the love of union, wee muft needs love our felves next and immediately, which is that thing wee defire to clofe and joyne with God; but others fecondarily, as thofe wee would have alfo participate of the fame good, and from this love, (the rule and meafure of our righteoufnes,) none are to be excluded, that are capable of God, and happineffe, becaufe the roote of love afwell to others as our felves, is God, the meafure of which is love to our felves, and therefore no particular enmity fhould interupt, therefore wee fhould love our enemies; You fee how wee have ftated, and whither wee have ledde this notion of righteoufnes, wee cannot leave it in a better place, and it was fit to fay fome what of that of which the word fayes fo much, and which armes fo faire and noble a part.

But how doth this peece arme the breaft, or how is it fitted thereunto? The breaft containes I told you the vitall parts, wherein properly as in the fubject, is the feate of life, that holines therefore, that righteouf-neffe, that image of God is wounded by unrighteouf-neffe; by finne, the Divell that wicked one fhoots at the faireft marke, and by unrighteoufnes wounds, that is it which drawes downe Gods wrath, puts a fting into every condition, into death it felf, that weakens the heart, makes timerous and fearefull; the breaft-plate in Greeke is Thorax, and they fay it is derived from Θωρεῖν, *hoc eft, fubfilite*, to leape or fhake, *Propter cordis palpitationem*, for the heart ever mooves, but un-righteoufnes and an evell confcience, makes it fhake inordinately, renders men timerous, and fearefull; now this peece of armour, this *breaft-plate of righteoufneffe* fecures you of this, thofe fhaking, thofe darting wounds,

R   and

and ads courage and affurance, fo Prov.28.1. *The wicked flyes when none purfues, but the righteous are bold as a Lyon,* now the ufe of armour is to render you, not onely fafe, but bold and fecure; Contrary to which are thofe feares, that make wicked men affraid of their owne fhaddowe, they goe without being driven, faving by their owne confcience, which is alfo excelently expreft, Lev.26. 36.37. *And upon them that are left alive of you, I will fend a faintneffe into their hearts in the Lands of their enemyes, and the found of a fhaking leafe fhall chafe them, and they fhall flee, as fleeing from a fword, and they fhall fall when none purfueth.*

And they fhall fall one upon another, as it were before a fword, when none purfueth, and yee fhall have no power to ftand before your enemies. Heere is a difpofition, quite contrary to fuch ftrength and courage, as this peece, *the breaft-plate of righteoufnes* gives, doe you not fee now need of an armour, when wickedneffe and unrighteoufnes brings you into that miferable condition; unrighteoufnes is oppofite to the being of a holy man, the renewed ftate of a man which *confifts in righteoufnes and true holineffe,* and to the comfort and welbeing of a faynt, which ftands as you have it, Rom.14.17. *In righteoufnes, peace, and joy in the Holy Ghoft;* marke the order, firft *righteoufnes,* which is as I may fay, the materiality of *peace,* and then *joy in the Holy Ghoft.* But may not the righteoufnes of Chrift, imputed by faith more properly be called, this peece of armour, then our owne inherent righteoufneffe or holineffe? Anfw. without all queftion, that is, the Roote and fource of all our righteoufneffe, Rom.8.3.4. *That the righteoufneffe of the law might be fulfilled in us, who walke not after the flefh, but after the fpirit.* That is, wee are reputed in Chrift to have fulfilled *the whole law,* for faies hee, *the righteoufnes of the law*

law is fulfilled in us ; there were two things the law required, a juſt ſuffering for what wee were in arreare, a due expiation for ſinne, and a perfect obedience, now in Chriſt wee are reputed to have done all this, *for Chriſt is the end of the law for righteouſneſſe, to every one that beleeveth,* Rom. 10.4. This was the firſt intention, and ſcope of the law videlizet, that Chriſt might juſtifie and bring men to life, by his obſervation and keeping of it, and therefore the Apoſtle blames them verſ. 3. *that being ignorant of Gods righteouſneſſe, they would eſtabliſh their owne righteouſneſſe,* by which meanes *they ſubmitted not to Gods righteouſnes,* that is, to that way that hee had ſet and ordained. But ſecondly, having made them righteous, and acquitted by imputation, and ſtanding right before God; God leaves us not thus, but the love of God producing in us, and upon us, ſome lovely effect, makes ſutable impreſſions and Charracters, to the relation wee hold to him, you have the print and Charracter of a ſonne upon you, aſwell as the relation of a ſonne, which is nothing els but a certaine image and likeneſſe of his holineſſe, and therefore if *you bee in Chriſt, you are a new creature,* 2. Cor. 5.17. Now how can any be a new creature, without the infuſion of new qualities, new guifts, without an eſſentiall change, for it is a new creation, therefore the ſcriptures deſcribes all the parts of this infuſed holineſſe, *yee were darkneſſe, but now yee are light in the Lord,* Eph. 5.8. alſo : *you have put on the new man, which is renewed in knowledge, after the image of him that created him,* Coll. 3.10. There is for your light, for your apprehenſions, you have another ſight of things then ever you have had, other lights, other notions. Alſo, you have a new heart, a new diſpoſition of ſpirit, another bent and frame, and propenſion, then you have had, ſo that of Ezek. 36.26.

I will

I will give you a new heart and a new spirit, and you are *to*
put on the new man, which after God is created in righteousnes
and true holinesse, Eph. 4. 24. Christ therefore that doth
all for us doth much in us, hee is a head of influence,
wee have him all among us, and every one hath him
all in their measure; and according to those influences,
and infusions, wee have our denominations, so *Abell*
was called righteous, so *Noah, Iob*, also *Zacharij & Elizabeth*,
Luk. 1. 6. *were both righteous before God, walking in all the*
ordinances and commandements of the Lord blamelesse. In this
sence a man may be called *Righteous*; that is, *regenerate*,
that is, *renewed*, although corruption remaines, as you
call a house white aswell as a Swan, though there be
many spots on it, and such a one may be said not *to sin*,
1 Joh. 3. 6. because hee is not given up to sin, but hath
his heart armed and fenced with a holy frame, and a
pursuite of righteousnesse. Now having thus distin-
guished, and explained things, this scripture in all the
parts and peeces of the armour, seemes rather to speake
of the working and motion of the graces of God in
us, then the imputation of Christs to us, which is that
which indeed gives the forme, *enargy*, and operation
to every peece; but because according to what Christ
is to us, so in a proportion, and according to our measure hee is in us, by his influence, by his infusions,
therefore wee are to till and improve him in us, and as
the divell could do nothing against us, but by virtue
of our corruptions; so Christ makes use of his owne
infusions, of his owne graces, of his workes in us, with
which through him, wee fight against the divell, so as
by the righteousnes of *Iesus Christ* infused into us, and
derived by his spirit, our vitall parts are armed, and secure against the divell, who by unholines, and unrighteousnes would destroy that building of Gods owne
rearing.   I have

I have bene some thing large in this, both in shewing you what righteousnes is, as it respects God and
man, and in distinguishing it from the imputed righteousnes of Christ, which is the temire wee hold by,
and by which wee stand accepted before God; and in
shewing you, how it secures you against sin, which is
the divells weapon to wounde us withall; If ye aske
mee how you shall put it on, in a word, *be renewed in the
spirit of your minde*, things are maintained, as they were
gotten, be converted often, one conversion is not
enough, the worke of repentance, that is, of a change
of heart, is of a continuall dayly use; you must *be
changed from glory to glory, as by the spirit of the Lord* righteousnes in you, acted, and enlarged by the spirit of
God, must worke out unrighteousnes in you, acted and
fomented by the divell, and you must do your part to
righteousnes, as you have done to sin, and *as ye have
yeilded your members servants to uncleannesse, and to iniquity
unto iniquity. So now yeild your members servants to righteousnes and to holinesse*, Rom.6.19. Your Members, that
is, your whole soule, the faculties of it, the endowments
of it must be yeilded in service to God, as they have
bene to sin and the divell, they must be now weapons
in Gods hand, under the command of his spirit, for so
saies hee ver.13. *neither yeild your members as weapons or
armes of unrighteousnes*, for so signifies the word, which
wee translate *instruments*: Wicked men, unrighteous
men furnish the divell with weapons to kill and destroy
themselves, their owne weapons slayes them, the
divell doth but helpe to point them and sharpen; but
wee must yeild our selves to God, *and our members, weapons of righteousnes to God*, and by doing this, *sin shall not
have dominion over you*, for saies hee, *yee are under grace, not
under the law*, that is, the grace of God in Christ, and

the

the affiftance of his fpirit will enable you to overcome fin, and the divell, which the law would never have done : Nothing hinders more then difcouragement, but feare not, imploy your members as weapons for God, and you will prevaile, the rigour of the law, Chrift hath fatisfied, and thofe parts which remaines you, which are left for you, grace will work in you, and by you, fo as let the divell be what hee will be ; *fin or unrighteoufneffe fhall not have dominion over you*, and confequently not the divell, againft whome ye fight, for hee moves in the ftrength of *unrighteoufneffe*.

We are come now to the third peece of armour, which is for the *feet and leggs*, for the *Breaft-plate* reached downe to the *knees*, and this covered the reft; by the feete are commonly denoted the *affections*, by which we martch or move to good, or ill, they are the movings and outgoings of the foule, and the feet and legs are a part, which needs afmuch armeing as any other thing, for in their motion to fight, they conflict with the difficulties of the place, and in their fightings are expofed to wounds and danger ; other parts are freed from that more, they are not fo much offended with the ground on which they are, but thefe are afwell expofed to the difficulties of the place, as to the wounds of the combate. The armour therefore for this part, is the *preparation of the Gofpell of peace*, that is, an ability and readines with chearfulneffe, to preach and confeffe the Gofpell.

Firft, that this is a great duty to confeffe, or manifeft upon all occafions, your beleefe of the Gofpell appeares by that place, Rom. 10. 10. *with the mouth confeffion is made to falvation* ; that is, it is a part of the duty which you owe to God, in order to your eternall falvation, to confeffe and promulge the glorious Gofpell

ſpell , which in your hearts you beleeve , for the faith
of the Goſpell ſhould ſo fire your heart, with the glory
of God, that the flame ſhould breake out ; On the contrary it is an abſurd and fooliſh thing , to talke of fire
where no flame or heate appeares , to ſpeake *of belee-*
ving to righteouſneſſe, where there is not at all occaſions,
a readineſſe to confeſſe with the mouth. This being
laid for a foundation , you ſhall ſee how two other places will helpe to interprete this. Thoſe *ſhooes*, the feet
armour, I take to be a fitneſſe and readineſſe to preach,
or declare the Goſpell of peace ; this ſemes to be ex-
tremely parrallelled , with Rom. 10.15. taken out of
Iſa. 52.7. *How beautifull are the feete of them that preach the*
Goſpell of peace, Heere you have the *Goſpell of peace* , the
ſame thing named in this place , and the bringing or
communicating of it expreſſed by feet. As heere by
the armour of the feet, but if any ſhall ſay this is onely
applicable to Miniſters , becauſe in the beginning of
this 15. *ver.* it is ſaid, *How ſhould they preach except they be*
ſent , that is utterly a miſtake , for by ſending there is
not meant , the particular and lawfull call of Miniſters,
which the Apoſtle heere treats not of, but imports
onely , that it is a ſpeciall ſigne of the love of God,
when the Goſpell is brought any whither, for hee ſends
it, it drops not out of the clouds, by chance or hazzard,
but it comes whither God ſends it, whither hee addreſ-
ſeth it, and therefore ſhould be received accordingly ;
The other place is, 1. Pet. 3.15. *Be ready alwaies to give*
an anſwere to every one of the hope that is in you. The word
ready is the ſame word , that is heere *prepared*, ἕτιμο,
and heere ἐπιμασία with a readines , or preparation,
having *your feet ſhod with a readineſſe of the Goſpell of*
peace; that is, as heere *with a readineſſe*, to give an account
of it , or preach it , or confeſſe it , as in the former
                                                    places,

places , as you have occasion , either by offering and
declaring it , or by answering and giving account *of*
the hope that is in you , of the Gospell the ground of that
hope , or of your actions according to that rule and
word ; you see how this exposition suits with a generall duty in other places commanded, and runnes para-
lell with the very phrases, and expressions of them, so
as the exposition falls naturally and without constraint.
If you aske mee now how this readines and preparation of preaching , and confessing the Gospell upon all
occations , armes the legs, and feet, which denotes our
Martches, and Motions in this warre against the divell.

1.   Answere first, because it imployes a great boldnes in
the faith of Christ , which fits for motion and going
forwards ; hee that is ready , and prepared to be a
Preacher, or Confesser, to give an account of his faith,
hath as it is said of the *Deacon, attained a good degree, and*
great boldnesse, and as Christ saith, *Hee that casts out divells*
in my name, will not lightly speake evill of mee ; so hee that is
ready and prepared to confesse and publish as hee hath
occasion, the Gospell of God is prepared for advance-
ing, for martching, for goeing forward; this therefore
it implyes, to wit, a boldnes of minde , and a courage.

2.   Secondly, the objections that the divell and wicked
men frame against our actions , and motions are extreamely hindering, make us heavy and timerous ; but
if you be able and ready to be a confessour, if yee can
preach or give account of it, and you be prepared to it,
you are safe enough , you will take any stepps , and
walke boldly , so as it is not onely a signe of courage as
before, but it doth actually and really inable you.

3.   Thirdly , to this you must adde what the Apostle
addes considerately, that it is *the Gospell of peace* , about
which, and for which you moove; this agrees extreamely well

ly well to this motion, for being to goe through many uneaven waies , and to breake through the thickeſt ranckes of enemies; you are helped by this, that you are at peace with God all the while, what ever enemies you meet with in the way , ſo as this Goſpell of peace fits you for motion, and by confeſſing , and promulgeing your faith, to conflict with others. So I ſtate this armour which the holy ſpirit appropriates to the legs and feet, I alter not the words of the Text, I ſhew you how it fits for motion :

The help is therefore to this peece of armour, is, firſt to be filled with right knowledge , *how can yee beleeve on him of whome yee have not heard, how can you preach him , how can you confeſſe him,* of whome ye are not well inſtructed, concerning whome you are not taught ; an implicite faith heere to beleeve as others doe , as your teachers doe, will not helpe you.

Secondly, you muſt be zealous, that will render you ready and prepared ; a zealous man wilbe communicating what hee hath , will have his confeſſions and anſweres at hand, when his Brothers darknes or ſcandall ſhall call for it , hee will put on for converting for enlightening of men , it will grieve him to ſee the world, and the divell gaine from God.

Thirdly, you muſt be poſſeſt with the peace I ſpoke of, *the Goſpel of peace,* will never come of from you, if your hearts be not filled *with peace* ; this is that Chriſt left his diſciples to worke with, and by. *Peace I leave with you , my peace ,* (that is, the peace of the Goſpell) *I give unto you,* ſo John. 16. 33. *Theſe things have I ſpoken unto you, that in mee ye might have peace. In the world yee ſhall have tribulation,* that is, you are to martch to heaven through a troubleſome world, the profeſſion and preaching of the Goſpell will coſt you much, but in Chriſt,

S   and

2.

3.

and in the Gofpell you fhall have peace ; The other is but outward, that is the moſt intimate peace, *a peace that paſſeth all underſtanding*, a peace that will enable you to goe to warre, and deny your ſelves of outward peace. How did this peace that made *Paul and Sylas ſing in the Priſon*, inable them to preach Chriſt abroade. What bold confeſſions could Stephen make in the midſt of all his enemies, upon the very point of Martirdome, when hee was at peace with *God*, and ſawe *Chriſt the King of peace at the right hand of God* ; It is not the enemye ſo much as the ſtrength or weakneſſe to reſiſt, and fight, that is confiderable if there be *more with you then againſt you* ; It is no matter what is againſt you, if you have a deepe and quiet peace within, it is no matter what noyſes you heare abroade. The Martirs that were filled with that peace in their ſharpe warfares, could ſay *non patimur ſed pati videmur*, we rather ſeme to ſuffer, then ſuffer indeed ; this will make you ſtrong in every motion towards fight, and this will ayde you to this profeſſion, and confeſſion of Chriſt, which will both aſſure all your owne motions, and by which as with ſpirituall feet, you doe move mightily againſt the divell.

Corrol. For the uſe of this inparticular, wee may confider how happy our conditions are, that wee are preachers and publiſhers of peace, *bleſſed are the peace makers*, and *how beautifull are their feet* ; this wee are if wee be filled with peace, *a peace that paſſeth all underſtanding, will paſſe its own bounds and fill others alſo.*

2. But then ſecondly, in a ſence wee are all preachers, all confeſſors, they that teach, muſt doe, and they that doe, muſt teach, that is by that doing, by the light of their actions which ſhines ; but in truth, wee ſhould not onely be contented to walke holily our ſelves, but wee

ſhould

should be ready and prepared to communicate what
ever wee have of the Gospell to others, as occasion
shall offer it selfe and draw it forth, which is both a
great motion and walke against the divell; and as it is
heer exprest, it armes our feet, and secures our motion
exceedingly in this warre, so as wee are not subject to
the shaking of objections, and disgraces which the
divell would represent to us, and cast in our way continually.

Thirdly, in this preaching and confessing the Gospell upon all occasions, doe it as the Gospell of peace,
bring it as the Angells did, who knew well the minde of
God, *Glory to God on high, on earth peace, good will towards
men,* Luk. 2. 14 *Also feare not, for behold, I bring you good
tydings of great joy, which shalbe to all people,* ver. 10. Offer
the Gospell like the Gospell, that is, like good newes,
the good newes of peace, let the world knowe that it
is brought and offred to all men, that it is good tydings
of great joy to all people : Christ is an universall
good, and as the heires of great kingdomes, are the
common possessions of all the subjects; so the Son
of the God of the whole earth, is good newes to all
mankinde, and it is pitty but that they should knowe
it, and that it should be offred to them, as it might be
their owne fault if they intertaine it not. And as
Christ said to his disciples, *when ye come into any house,
say peace be to it.* It is time enough for your peace to
returne to you, when they refuse to receive you. This
if any thing will take with the guilty world, who from
the sence of their owne ill are a thousand times apter
to dispaire, then beleeve, or at least to be hardened in
a negligent desperate way : This will also make good
the ends of the Gospell, which are the glory of Christ,
and the alluring, and gaining of the elect; and a soule

gained

gained by the freeft way of grace, will vent its obedience by love, and this will put honour upon your
felves, render your feete beautifull, render you accep-
table and defireable, where ever you come in the world,
when *you fhalbe fhod with the fhooes of the preparation of
the Gofpell of peace.*

4.   Fourthly, as ye are to make after much knowledge,
for a cleare rule of all your actions, and ftepps, even to
a readineffe to confeffe it, and preach it; for that is the
preparation heere meant, that yee may bee in a readineffe, fo when you are in fuch a preparation, walke
boldly, let the world fee by your walking and your
motion, and fteddines that jou are armed, when you can
paffe through foule waies, *good report and ill report*, when
ye walke among thornes, tread upon Serpents and Adders, *and
they fhall not hurt you.* Paul fure had his hand well
armed, when the viper dropt from it without hurting
him, fo it is a figne you are well armed, when yee feare
no wayes into which providence fhall leade you, and
when you come of without hurt, though there be
pikes and ftakes in the way, ye are not pierced; this
walking by example, and as occation is by voyce, by
confeffion, or preaching, will make many followers,
you will become leaders your felves, and that will be a
glorious walkeing, when yee fhall not onely treade
hard Pathes, but lead up troopes, wee fee even bruit
beafts in motion are put on by the voyce as well as by
example, or any other way : Let the world know that
warre is but the Vizard, but there is peace within, un-
derneath : Let them know that there are fweets and
rofes, though they fee nothing outwardly but thornes,
and Bryars, your walking fteddily will fhew that your
felves are armed, and your example and voyce together, will have a great influence upon others, to be
                                                    fure

sure a readinesse and preparednesse to confesse the Gospell of peace, will arme you for all the hard martches, and what ever the divell shall object in your way.

Wee are come to the fourth peece of Armes, which is a Shield fitted not so much to any one part, (as the other peeces) as to the whole, for it is moveable, and propper to keepe of at a distance, & this is faith : Now this *above all things is* to be taken up, that is, *Especially*, this is the most considerable peece of Armour you have; Some reade it *in all things*, that is, with every peece of Armour, yee must mingle faith, with *Truth*, with *Righteousnesse*, with the *Preparation of the Gospel of Peace:* or referre it to temptations, that is, you must oppose faith to every temptation, which is true; but I rather thinke it is meant heere, *Especially*, that is, to say above all things in a more especiall manner, *Take unto you the Shield of faith*, like that place Coll. 3. 14. where the same word is used, *And above all things but on Charity*, so as though every peece of Armour be very considerable, yet none like *the shield of faith*, and hee gives you the reason, because by it *you shall be able to quench the fiery darts of the Divell*, who for his superabundant malice and wickednes hee calls *the wicked one*, that is, who with the greatest and most intense height of wickednesse pursues God and Man, but especially, good men the Saints; And yee shall not quench, some of his darts onely, but all his darts, hee hath enough of them, hee hath of all kindes, this shield will receive them, and repell them all; Hee tells you also, of what kinde they are, *They are fieri darts*, his Arrowes are poysoned Arrowes, they do not onely wound as Iron and steele doth, but there is a Poyson, a burning in them, of an ill quality, hard to cure, hard to be quenched; but now the holy Ghost prescribes you a remedy,

an Armes fitted on purpose as they are darts , *faith as a
shield* shall repell them , as they are *poyfoned and fiery*;
faith as Water, or Balfome, or Oyle, *shall Quench* , by
faith ye shall be enabled to *Quench* them: Faith properly
as a shield doth not quench but repell, but faith enables
you; that is , there is a mighty power and operation
in faith , doeing that which nothing els can doe , that
as yee have falves , properly to draw out stings , or
thornes , and as yee have Balfomes, to take out fire and
poyfon , to quench and destroy the malignity of a
poyfoned dart, fo you have faith fitted and proportio-
ned to *quench the fiery darts of the wicked* , your greateft
enemy, and who shoots continually, and therefore are
they called *all his fiery darts* ; hee wants not Ammuni-
tion, hee need not feare for want of Powder , hee hath
great and curfed abilities , and a fpirit fitted to act
them alwayes ; but faith can deale with him, and render
all his dartings vaine, and of no effect. You fee now the
full meaning of thefe words , and of how great a confideration faith is , to this warre , fo as from the reafon
of the thing which the Apoftle gives , it deferves an
Emphefis, *An above all;* that is, efpecially want not this,
as Sallomon faies of wifedome, *Above all gettings get
underftanding* , and *keepe thy heart with all dilligence,* fo
above all things take the shield of faith. Before wee
confider more particularly , of this fo much commended faith, wee will thinke a little what thofe fiery darts
are, which are to be received, and quenched by faith; by
fiery darts heere, I underftand not fo much temptations
to all kindes of him , though faith ferves for all meets
with them alfo, but the *Breaft-plate of righteoufneffe* femes
propper alfo for them , but fome *fiery* envenomed im-
poyfened darts , to which nothing but *the shield of faith*
can be oppofed ; faith will fecure you in all things
                                          afwell

afwell as other peeces of armour, but efpecially faith is of ufe heere; And thefe darts feme to be either fome burning vyolent temptations to lufts, or after them to difpaire: For the firft, our natures fince the firft defilement by orriginall corruption, were never per-fe&ly coole, it is by fome principle within us, that Sathan workes upon us, our natures are ftuble and tinder; there is a great deale of combuftible matter within us, which the wicked one knowes well enough, and therefore fhoots his Granadoes, his fire-workes, his fiery darts, if wee were Ice and Snow, if we were per-fe&ly coole and cold, to lufts, the divell would not loofe his paynes nor his darts, but being fiery our fel-ves, apt to burne, hee flings in fire, fiery darts, and wee are inftantly and prefently, in a flame, like charcoale burnt already, or ftuble prepared already for burning by the funne; fo hee did to David in the cafe of Bath-fheba, though hee were a good man, tooke him at an advantage, when his corruptions were moft fiery, neereft burning, when idleneffe, fecurity and peace, had dryed and heated him to lufts, and vanity, then hee flung in a fiery dart, and the flame was unquenchable. The like hee did with *Amnon*, who having received the fiery dart, was fo vexed that hee fell ficke for his fifter *Tamar*, 2.Sam. 13. 2. and was fo deftroyed with that flame, as hee never ceafed till hee counted *folly in Ifrael*: in wayes moft barbarous and wicked, both in the profecution of his love, and in his abufing and reje&ing of her afterwards, and the one was as *fiery* as the other, *hee hated her* now *more then hee had loved her*, ver.15. the love was without meafure, fo was the ha-tred; fo are men ftung with *the fiery darts of the divell*, there is nothing but extreames, no Mediocrity, all is without meafure, and then for a little of that they call pleafure;

pleafure, they have a world of paine, and gall, and bit-
ternefſe; which is the other fiery darts, made way for by
lufts, and that is difpaire; for I ſhould thinke that in
this inſtance, the inhumanity and barbaroufneſſe of
Amnon afterwards to his ſiſter, came from the terrour
and confufion of his confcience, *what fruit had you of
thofe things whereof you are now aſhamed*, Rom. 6. 21. After
the ſin is committed, ſhame and horrour ceazeth prefently, which hurryes the minde ordinarily as faſt to
difpaire as it did before, to the countinent of the luſt;
therefore luſts ſhould be lookt upon, as they are goeing
not as they are comeing, or as they are promifing,
peracto ſcelere magnitudo ejus conſpicitur, as Tacitus inferres
of Nero, after hee had killed his Mother, therefore
wee ſhould looke on ſin with that eye, which within a
few howers wee ſhall ſee them; and this is the ſecond
head of the fiery darts I told you of, namely inections
to difpaire, how many after the commiſſions of Murthers, Adulteryes, Treatheryes, have bene confumed
and likt up, by thefe fiery darts, and brought to miferable ends, under the notion of difpaire: What thinke
you of *Spira*, who for a little ſhrincking and retracting
his confeſſion, the profeſſion of the Gofpell I told
you of, eſteemed the flames of hell leſſe then thofe hee
felt, and wiſht himfelfe often there that hee might
knowe the difference; What thinke you before him of
Iudas, who found no reſt, no quiet of ſpirit, but in the
Gallowes, hee was utterly druncke up by difpaire, and
went downe quicke to his owne place. But the ſaints
feele thefe fiery darts, as David did for luſting, ſo him-
ſelfe alſo and divers others for difpairing, therefore
hee ſaies, *Hee roared all the day, and his foule, and his bones
were fore vexed, and his eye, his foule & his Belly were confumed*,
and the divell heerein takes the advantage of ſome outward

ward lowenesse and depression of condition, either in body, or estate, or reputation, or some melancholy of body, or constitution, which is a temper easily fired to extremities; and that the Saints have their fyering to lustings, or dispaire aswell as others, whether they be of things bulky in themselves or little.

But, what kinde of faith is it that you must oppose to these burnings, to these *fiery darts,* and how doth faith relieve you? *Object.*

Certainely it is no other then that by which you be-leeve God, to be yours in Christ. *Ans.*

The *Shield* here spoken of is taken from the simili-tude of a *Doore,* such as were the largest shields, it must be large enough to shield the whole body:

And secondly, as a shield it must receive the darts and repell them, and quench the fire before it reach the body, before it incorporate it selfe with the minde, and enter as it were into the substance of the spirit, for then there will be more tearing and difficulty to get it out.

But how doth faith doe this?

First and especially as it calls God, God in Christ to our ayde. When the Divell shoots his *fiery Darts,* either for lusting, or dispairing, it is not for flesh and blood to oppose it selfe, your mortalities, your resolutions, your reasonings will prove combistible matter, and be burnt up, be burnt away, and your spirit will be left fiered, and empoysoned by those Darts. The Dart will sticke, & it will be worke to get it out; Now in this case faith leads you directly to God, & sets God against the Divell, so as the combate by the wisdome of faith, is changed, and made now rather betweene God and the Divell, then betweene you and the Divell, & the Divell which could have subdued you easily, fals under God

T present-

prefently, *This is that ftronger then hee that bindes the ftrong man and cafts him out.* This was Davids way, *From the ends of the earth will I cry to thee, when my heart is overwhelmed, Leade mee to the Rocke that is higher then I, Pfal.61.2.* that is where ever I am, or where ever thou art, as thy fpirit can finde mee out , fo I will finde thee out, *When I am overwhelmed, when I am greatly in diftreffe, I will cry to thee*, as a child doth to his father, that is fet upon by one ftronger then himfelfe, cries out to his father and trufts to his ftrength; *Set mee upon a Rocke*, or *thou wilt fet mee upon a Rocke*, that is, it is fo high, as I cannot reach it without thou fet mee upon it, or *higher then I*, that is, above my owne ftrength, or my owne abilities, even upon thy felfe and thy fonne, where I may be fafe, for in cafe of *overwhelmings*, in cafe of *fiery Darts*; there is no other way but to fet God, as yours, as one in covenant with you, your all, and friends againft the Divell, *to ftand ftill and fee the falvation of God*, when the red fea was before, and the Egyptians behinde, what could the Ifraelites doe, (in that cafe there was no way for wifedome or ftrength to make through). *But ftand ftill and fee the falvation of God*, cafting all upon God, and difparing in themfelves altogether.

2.   But fecondly, this fhield of faith can relieve you in this extremity by outbidding fights (as in a fecond and under way) againft all luftings it can oppofe prefently the recompence of the reward, and ye have a luft for that alfo: So Mofes was not without the luftings of ambition and vaine glory, to be called *the Son of Pharoahs Daughter*, but the eye which hee had, to the recompence of reward, outbids them infinitely, and therefore hee chofe rather afflictions which no man would fimply chufe: So *Chrift for the glory fet before him*, indured and fuffered any thing, a lively faith realizeth
things,

things, and makes them prefent ; faith will tell you
prefently when a fiery luft affaults you , yeild not, and
in ftead of pleafing your flefh, or your humour , which
is paffing, you will pleafe Chrift, you will pleafe your
confcience, and that pleafure is fweet indeed , that remaines ; nay you fhall heare of this againe , this fighting , this quenching, fhall come into your reward , in
fuch times and in fuch things , wherein you would be
moft of all confidered. And againft the burnings of
difpaire as in a fecond way , alfo faith will fhewe the
riches of mercy, the merrits of the blood of Chrift, and
will tell you that it is difhonourable to God to judge
his goodnes , leffe then your wickedneffe , or that the
merrits of Chrift cannot hold ballance with your finning , will fhewe you as great difproportion betweene
grace and fin, as betweene God and you, will make (in
a word) difpaire wicked in nothing as in the unreafona-
bleneffe of it.

But then thirdly , as an effect of both thefe, faith   3.
fuckes and drawes downe the dew of the fpirit , the
cooling waters , the refrefhing ftreames , if need be
balfome, and oyle, to quench the fire before it kindle,
or to fetch it out; when your concupifcents are cooled,
by the Holy Ghoft, and your fpirit is in temper , *Fiery
darts* will do no hurt , as a Grannado that falls into a
Pit of water , there is fire in it , but before the blowe
gives it is quencht: O thofe fweet & cooling influences of the fpirit , how refrefhing are they , as dewe to
thirfty grounds ; when *Dives* burned , what would hee
have given for fome water, to coole his tongue. When
wicked men are fiered by the divells darts, to difpaire
or luft, or perfecution , their owne fpirits are inflamed , burnt up , and they burne what ever they come
neere, and fo they muft till they be utterly confumed,

      for

for there is no heavenly dewe, no water, no rayne, no balſome, no droppings of the ſpirit : But to us there is a *River*, *the ſtreames whereof ſhall make glad the City of God*, Pſal.46.4. Shall refreſh us, ſhall keepe us from burning, and fyering, and chapping, and hee gives an account of it, ver.5. *God is in the midſt of her*, *ſhee ſhall not be greatly mooved*; there is the head of that fountaine, hee will not ſuffer the divell to gaine upon you, to waſte you, to drinke you up, very much to fire you, but the ſtreames ſhall continually refreſh you, and make you glad, when others ſhalbe like the parched heath in the wilderneſſe eaſily inflamed, a curſe to themſelves and others.

Coroll.

    Therefore with all gettings gett faith, *above all take the ſhield of faith*, and take it as I have told you , take it on like a large ſhield , that it may be fitt to cover you, beleeve not ſcantily, beleeve not a little, have not your faith to fetch, and prove, and ſpell, when the fiery Darts are ſhooteing, how will you make this uſe of it els, that I have told you; is there any thing the divell would rob you of ſo much as lively faith, effectuall faith, bold and hardy faith, hee knowes why well enough, it will repell his fiery darts, it will quench them, yeild him not that peece of armour in any proportion , that is ſo dammageable to him, and ſo neceſſary for you ; faith is uſefull in every thing , but in theſe caſes, faith doth not all (as I have told you) and while you are doing this, the obedience of faith , the uſe of faith is as pleaſing to God, as reſiſting the fiery dart is neceſſary for you ; as therefore ye would be relieved when you moſt need it , when your ſoules are fyered with luſt or diſpaire, when thoſe flames drinke up your ſpirits , and undoe you, beleeve boldly, beleeve ſtrongly, without if's and and's, have God tyed and made one with you, by faith according to the right notion of it, and then dread nothing,

thing, heere is good newes for you, you will be *able to quench all the fiery Darts of the wicked;* There now remaines nothing but some helpes to take this *shield of faith.*

First, consider it under the notion of obedience in it, the worke of God and the will of God is ingaged, you may be bold with your selves, (and yet yee cannot because ye are creatures, ye are not your owne) but will you be bold with the will of God : This to those that have but a little faith, and love already will be a great argument. God bids you sanctify his name, bids you honour your father, &c. you will do it, why ? because it is a thing not left to your choice; God bids you sanctify him by beleeving, honour him by beleeving, and this is first to God, to God immediately: I beseech you, looke not on faith in this notion, as a priviledge left to the arbitration of your owne wills, whether you will be so good to your selves or no, but as an indispensible duty : Some duties may be dispensed with for ends, as the worship of God in some of his ordinance, but this dutie lies so hard upon you, as it is not to be dispensed with all for a moment, not for the greatest good, not for the salvation of all men; if God be great to you, therefore obey him in beleeving, or upon the same reason, cast of all Religion and disobey him in every other thing, but if you feare to doe that, then knowe that the same God, that bidds you doe any other thing, bids you also beleeve, and know that this commandement is the least arbitrary of all the rest.

Secondly, consider what obstructs faith, if negligence, and want of consideration, as that doth much, and often, I beseech you let mee set you on considering : consider that you will goe to hell without it, if you will not beleeve God for the pardon of your sinnes, and that hee is yours in Christ, beleeve him for

1.

2.

this, that without this you wilbe condemned for ever,
God may feme to put it to your choice, whether you
will beleeve or no; but hee doth by no meanes put it
to your choice, whether you will goe to hell or no, if
you beleeve not, for that is determined with him, *that
the fearefull and unbeleevers* fhalbe caft into hell, and indeed thither are all men goeing a pace, onely belief
turnes the motion, and makes the earth affend upwards.

But if you fay you fee, you fee your mifery enough
in unbelief, but ye want boldnes to beleeve, that you
thinke that there is no proportion betweene fin and
fuch a nothing as faith is, there is a proportion betweene fin and damnation, but not betweene fin and
faith: right now I have you where I would, but then
confider that the things wherin God ufeth man in the
way to falvation, are indeed nothing, or as nothing,
by the *foolifhneffe*, that is, by the *Nothingneffe* of *Preaching hee faves them that beleeve*; The *Veffells* in which his
word comes, are *earthen*, as good as nothing, *our righteoufnes reacheth not to him*, and though our reward be
heaven, yet our merrit is nothing, juft nothing: And
therefore if faith in refpect of its owne internall vallew, or as a grace in this cafe, were any thing, wee
fhould never be faved by it, but now our comfort and
affurance is that it is nothing. But on the contrary,
though there be no proportion betweene fin and faith,
yet there is a proportion betweene fin and Chrift, or
if you will have mee fpeake the truth, there is no proportion in this regard; Chrifts dyeing, Chrifts fuffering, makes fin nothing, fo that that which held the
greateft proportion, before God, before, and was
heavyer then the fand of the fea, deeper then hell, is
now nothing: what will you thinke your debts greater
                                                    then

then God can pay, will you ballance your wickednes and his love, your unkindnes may be aggranated, and made greater by his love, but it cannot be made even with his love, for hee is God; In a word, wee cannot out-fin his pardon, or grace, by any thing but unbeliefe, fo as this littleneffe, this nothingnes of faith, is your advantage, becaufe in this great bufineffe of our falvation God will be all in all, and you fhall thanke your felves for nothing : Did it hinder Naaman the Affirian, that to wafh in Jordan was nothing, or did it relieve Jericho, that the bloweing of Rams-hornes was nothing, if it had bene any thing, it had not done it, for God is refolved to deftroy Jericho by nothing, that is, by himfelfe alone; and therefore he will have you by nothing, or by that which is as good as nothing, in refpect of what you doe: But on the other fide, hee findes enough in the ballance, to make your fins nothing, even his owne eternall love, and the fuffering and merrits of his owne fon.

Thirdly, Gods heart is in this matter of faith, never any thing was fo fenced with mottineffe, with threats, and commands, with intreatings and invitings, with words and oathes, with fignes and feales, with rewards and punifhments. The Gofpell is nothing but the Meffage of faith, Chrift himfelf and all his Minifters, but the preachers of faith. The great bufineffe is to make the match, to tye the knott betweene God and our foules, the reft, other things, flow on naturally : Love followes faith, works flowe from love. *But without faith, its impoffible to pleafe God,* without faith wee are *Strangers and a farre of.* Now that which is fo neere Gods heart, and fo advantagious to our felves, wee fhould doe, wee fhould be much in what ever the divell fay, to the contrary, God never hedged any thing about

3.

like

like this, never any thing came fo freely off, the making of this coft him his Minifters ordinances and feales, and without it all is nothing.

4.   Fourthly, to fetch Arguments, not onely from necef-fity and duty, & reafon, but ingenuity, the onely falve you can apply to the wounds of Chrift, is beleeving, your fins made them your faith heales them, *Hee fhall fee of the travaile of his foule, and be fatisfied*, Ifa. 53.11. That is, hee hath beene at a great deale of paines and coft ; now what are his in-comes, what will make up this poore people for whome hee did, and fuffered, all this will truft him and beleeve in him, for fo it followes, *by his knowledge, fhall my righteous fervant juftify many*, that is, by the knowledge and beliefe of him, they fhalbe jufti-fied, this fatisfies him, this payes him, this is the onely way you have to make him amends ; Now his ftripes hath healed you, heale him by your faith, do a little nobly, and freely for him, that hath done fo much for you, fticke not with him to beleeve him, that ftuck not to dye for you.

5.   But then laftly, did the divell never let loofe any fiery darts upon you, or may hee not doe it, if hee have not, yee can judge the leffe what it is to want this fhield, but aske Judas, and hee will tell you, aske David hee will tell you, aske Paul when Sathan buffet-ted him, and hee had nothing but God to relie upon ; If hee have, I hope experience will make us wife to have our fhield ready, if hee have not knowe that hee may doe, looke that hee will doe, and will doe it, when you are weakeft, when you are loweft, provide for that evill day, get up your *fhield*; this *of faith in God through Chrift*, *as yours*, and then when hee comes, what have you to doe, ye can turne God loofe to him, yee can fetch downe liquor and vertue of that temper and coolenuffe,

cooleneſſe, as ſhall dead and quench and extinguiſh his
darts, and in the thing wherein hee is proud and
mighty, you will be above him, and to hard for him.

We are come in the fifth place to another peece of
the great and ſure armour, with which the ſpirit of
God armes us againſt the divell, a peece for our head,
the Helmet of ſalvation, as that before was more generall applicable to the whole Body.

That by this *Helmet* is meant *hope*, the Apoſtle who
is his owne beſt interpreter tells you 1. Theſſa. 5. 8. *And*
for an Helmet the Hope of Salvation : This peece of armour is of excellent uſe, and proper to that part it
defends ; The worth of it appears as by many things:
So by the deplorable condition of thoſe that want it,
they *have no hope* (ſaies hee) and *they are without God in*
the world, Eph. 2. 12. they wanted that ligament, that
tye to faſten them to God, and ſo were left moſt miſerable.

Wee muſt conſider a little, what *hope* is, and then,
why it is called *of ſalvation*, and then how it fits that
part, to which it is deſtined, and doth the worke of an
Helmet.

It is a receiv'd maxime, that *all affections are rooted in*
love, and as they are rooted in love, ſo they are acted by
love, even hatred and malice it ſelfe, hath its riſe in
ſome thing loved, for therefore I hate ſuch a thing,
becauſe I love the contrary : Againe as affections are
rooted in love, and acted by love, ſo love is felt, and
appeares according to the affection it acts by, and is
ſeene through that, as the ſunne which is alwayes the
ſame in it ſelfe, yet workes upon us according to the
conſtellations it poſſeſſeth, and the light coulours it
ſelf, according to the body through which it ſhines,
ſo loves workes and appeares much according to the

affection

affection it possesseth, and through which it renders it self visible, for example :

Love appeares very darke in sorrow , violent in choller, tranquill and peaceable in joy, dejected in dispaire, but in hope love is in its Throne , there it appeares in most pompe , there it workes with most efficacy , and is altogether lovely.

This affection of all others semes to be destined to great affaires, and hath a mighty influence either upon our doeing, or suffering.

It was all that Alexander had to inable him to the conquest of the world , distributing all his other goods that hee had received from his father ; Againe what is it but this that makes men every day crosse the seas , labour the ground , seeke after Mines in the bowells of the earth, fight , and pursue victories , nay it is that which accompanyes men to the scaffold, and to their death bedds.

But to follow our methods , wee consider not hope heere , in that loose sence, in which it is commonly taken, namely for a certaine fault, and lowe attendancy, or lookeing after some good thing desired, and so to be before faith, and without it , as when wee are apt to say , I cannot beleeve such a thing , but I hope it well; but on the contrary we take it for a firme expectation of some future good, which wee doe already beleeve, and are assured of, so saith the scripture Heb. 11.1. *Faith is the substance of things hoped for.* Gal. 5.5. *Wee waite for the hope of righteousnesse by faith*, that is, faith gives you the ground of waiteing , which is by hope, *so if wee hope wee waite*, Rom. 8.25. so as this hope which must be our *Helmet* is a superadded grace to faith , a birth and effect of it.

It is called , *the Helmet of Salvation* , for salvation is
the

the great thing about which faith and hope is conver-
fant, fo faith Paul, *receiving the end of your faith, the falvation
of your foules,* fo *the hope of falvation,* becaufe, that, as the
greateft, conteynes all other inferiour goods, and in
the eyeing and profecution of which by faith and hope
wee fecure our felves the moft abundantly.

But how doth this Armour fit the part, it is deftined for, and doe the worke of an *Helmet.*

The head is as it were the principle of action, and
of our intentions, as the head governes and directs
the members, fo our end and intention, which is our
Simbolicall head, being the principall and rife of all
our actions, that which gives vigour and activity to
them, had need of fome peece of armour for its defence, which the Apoftle heere makes to be *the hope of
Salvation.*

Now this *Helmet* doth its worke thus, the world and
Sathan that they might poyfon the fountaine, corrupt
our ends, and our intentions, would bribe us with
fomething outward, and fenfuall, and therefore holds
over our heads many things to tempt and allure us, futable to our fences, and corrupted nature, offers us
crownes of applaufe, allures us with pates of pleafure
(falfely fo called) and to makes thefe rellifh, to take the
better, terrifies us with thorny paths, and ill conditions, in holy wayes, with perfecutions, and fcornes,
gives you the choice of crownes of thornes, and gold,
but both flefhly and carnall ; the Holy Ghoft now
gives you *for an Helmet the hope of Salvation,* holds that
over your head toward of thefe blowes, and thofe
affaults, and what is that ? The affured expectation and
waiting for of eternall glory, for fo it is called in other
places, *The hope of eternall life, the hope of glory,* Rom. 5.2
and Tit.3.7. Firft, hope in its nature and definition is

V 2   the

the waiting for , and expectation of a good thing,
which makes it a pleafant, and releeving affection, becaufe the object of it is good , not as griefe , nor as
feare , which hath for its object an ill thing ; But our
hope which is our *Helmet* , wards and guards our heade,
it is made up of the beft and moft futable good , it is a
good comprehending all other goods , and therefore
called *falvation* in the abftract , it is a glorious good, for
it is *the hope of glory* , and for duration it is not earthly,
fenfuall , and paffing , but it is *eternall life an eternall*
weight of glory.

2.   Secondly , hope is of good things to come , and
therefore it is an expectation , for *hope that is feene is not*
hope, for what a man fees , why doth hee yet hope for ? Rom. 8.
24. So as it is a pleafant paffing your time, in the expectation of a defired good ; But now the difference will
lie not onely in the degree of good , for ours is of
things eternall, but in the degree of expectation, wordly
hopes are founded upon fuch fleight bottomes, as they
contribute not much to comfort , in regard of which
fome have called hope a dreame , which prefents it
felfe to wakeing men , and from thence it is faid, *that*
the Hipocrites hope perifheth ; but our hope is of another conftitution , for it is grafted upon faith which
gives a certainty , and reality to the thing , fo as no
feare of faileing fhall weaken or impaire your hope, but
hope fhall ftand upon a fure bottome , and pleafantly,
and joyfully expect what already by faith is made
moft fure to us.

    To fpeake a little more , a little more particularly
of this affection, it is of a good thing, abfent, difficult
and poffible , I have fhewed you how our hope is con-
verfant about the beft and higheft good , the abufe of
this affection (for that will helpe to fhew the ufe of it)
lies

lies in pitching it upon things that are not good ; In truth all other things, but spirituall, God, heaven, and eternity , have no other vallue , but what ignorance and a lye puts upon them , opinion indeed gives them a name , honours them with a title which they deserve not, and yet how much doe outward things ingage this affection : Honour which depends upon the opinion of others, which is extreamely passing , and perishing, which is the reward oftentimes of crimes , which are succesfull, and glitter, and pleasures which are accompanied with regret , and shame , and followed with grief; And riches ordinarily , the object of the basest mindes , and men ; All these things , and what ever more is outward , are but the shadowes and pictures of good ; As in a picture you thinke you see the birds flye, men standing of from the cloath , but when you come neere it, there is nothing but the lynes of a pensil, nothing but markes upon a cloath or table , and so are these things, nothing but shadowes, pictures, dreames, they must have a light proper to shew them by , false lights , yet these are the objects of the hopes of the greatest part of men.

Againe , these things as they are not good enough, so they are not absent enough for hope , for though things of sence are not ever in the possession of them which most make after them, yet they are amongst us, they are in the world , but this hope carries us properly beyond every thing. *The eye sees , and the eare heares, and what enters into the heart of man.*

Againe, things that are the object of hope are difficult, but difficult and worthy, or great in a right sence, are of an equall extent , to labour in the smoake and mudd , for smoak and mudd it may be difficult , but it is a difficultie without worth, it is base and meane, and

so hath

so hath nothing in it of great, or worthy, in which re-spect onely difficult things should be undertaken.

Then, how often doth hope mis-applyed ingage in impossibilities, and so becomes a meere imposture to us. How often are men befooled heere, and in their desires, and hopes (which actuate those desires) pursue impossible things. Men foolishly thinke that miracles should be wrought in their favour, and the whole order of the universe changed for their sakes, men that merit the gallowes hope for a pardon, not because they have any assurance of the judges favour, or because their faults are pardonable, but because they would live: and which is ridiculous, old men that are so in extremity, hope for an old age yet to come.

I have shewed you already that our hope which is our Helmet, is of good things, a good that wants a name, good enough to expresse it, and therefore is called *salvation*, a name abstract, and comprehensive to the utmost.

Againe, I have shewed, that it is of good things to come, and heerein it differs from faith, for faith sees them as it were present, and therefore it is *the substance of things hoped for*, but hope lookes upon them, (as indeed they are) at a distance; In a word, faith gives you the assurance, Hope the expectation.

Againe difficult they are, and great and difficult, worthie and difficult, accordingly, they cost Christ much, and they cost us much, so difficult, as for the attaining of them, God must come out of heaven, Christ must die and suffer: God must set all his wise-dome on worke, that wee may have a ground to pitch our hopes upon, and for our part, hope is mannaged and conversant about difficult things, as ye shall heare.

But

But then laſt of all, our hope is wiſe, the things are poſſible about which it is converſant, ſo poſſible, as they are aſſured, and therefore its called *the full aſſurance of Hope*, Heb.6.11.

Let us knowe then where wee are, and what uſe *Coroll.* wee have of this affection; The truth is Chriſtian Religion, is altogether founded upon hope, the things of this life are not our portion, wee breath after what is to come, let us therefore live as men, untyed from this world, and faſten to another by hope, let the pleaſures and honours, and profits of this world be dead things to us, becauſe wee have no hope to animate them; Hope acts and animates above any thing, but wee want this engine, becauſe we have not that object. For inſtance, to appeare ſomething, to be great, wiſe, and honourable, is the great contention, and purſuite of this world: *When Chriſt who is our life ſhall appeare, then ſhall wee appeare, &c.* Heavenly hope puts you off thither, and diſputes not the thing, but the time, ye ſhall have enough of appearing, but it ſhalbe in a peculiar and advantageous time, *when Chriſt ſhall appeare* to fill up his triumph, to adorne that pompe, reſpite your deſire of appearing till then; God doth but time it for us, ſo for pleaſures to enjoy your ſelves, to be ſatisfied, to be at eaſe, to gratify and content every part of you, theſe are mens hopes, one time or other you ſhall get it; There is a place of pleaſures, *the preſence of God*, and there is a fullneſſe and compleatneſſe of pleaſure, but it is in that place and in other, *and there are plaſures for evermore*, pleaſures that are as long as they are great, but it is at the right hand of God; The pleaſures Sathan would give you are of a baſe alloey, their durance is but of that minute in which they are enjoyed; Their fullneſſe is worſe then

their

their emptinesse, for they are not onely vaine, falling
short of that good they promised, but vexing also, and
deceiving, the truth is, this is not a life for pleasures,
but for paines, especially to Christians, and so saies
the Apostle, *If in this life onely wee have hope, wee are of
all men most miserable.* If our hopes (as other mens) were
heere, wee were in a worse condition then they, that
cannot eate their meates, and enjoy their comforts,
tast of their daintyes, partly, because there is a greater
disproportion betweene us and them, then betweene
they and them, and partly, because our light and our
conscience is to much raised, & of too great a tender-
nesse to digest their morsells; what then have wee nothing to ballance their contentments? not to speake
of other things, what ever returnes faith and hope can
make wee have, *They are without hope*, wish them joy of
what they have, but hope they have none; and this let
mee tell you, improve this well, and it shall pay all the
charges of their gaines, you have *the hope of eternall life,
the hope of glory*, of what ever your hearts can wish and
desire: Faith gives things a footing and a subsistance, &
hope is grafted upon it, and is ready by the expectation
of better things, to outbidd the world, and by virtue
of a pleasure taken in things to come, to carry you a-
bove the false pretensions of pleasure which the world
makes ofter, therefore content your selves with your
portion, and use your Helmet to ward of the assaults
of semeing goods or ills, as Sathan shall present them.

But more particularly, use hope for joy, for patience
for workeing, live in the joy of hope, let one spirituall
affection inprove and provoke another, that there is
a joy of hope, appeares in this, which wee usually say
of worldly hopes, that things are usually better in the
hopes, then in the enjoyment, and wee see men will
fell

sell any thing rather then their hopes : Now those hopes in comparison with ours, have two or three notable defects.

First they are built upon uncertainties and contingenties, they have no firme bottome, and ground work, and so cannot be intire, cannot be without the mixture of feare, feare of issue, feare of successe, and this let mee adde, that the more they hope, the more they will feare, out of a loathnesse to want the good things they desire, and so it is a mixt affection, that prickes, and pinches aswell as relieves, and comforts. Worldly men enjoy litle their hopes, or their possessions, not their possessions, for they are ballanced with uncertainties, and emptinesse, so as they are faine to relieve themselves, by their hopes, by their reachings after more, nor their hopes, doe they enjoye purely and sincerely, for they are mixt with feare, which oftentimes is the weightiest ingredient, and beares the greatest part of the composition; but our hopes have not this impediment to joy, but on the contrary carry evidence and subsistance with them, being built upon the evidence and subsistance of faith, so that what faith firmely beleeves, hope joyfully expects, and waites for; What is the great happines of heaven, but the fixeing & stayeing of joyes by eternity : Now the joy of that hope is fixed by faith, which gives it a steddy and untottering foundation, so that what you have, you have ; If joy come in by that doore, it will or ought to do so alwaies, there is no rationall or necessary mixture of feare, because there is no rationall cause of doubting.

Secondly, there is a vanity of *rejoycing in boastings*, as James saith, and so an evill, *for all such rejoycing is evill:* The mixture of feare is a troublesome, but it is a rationall

X nall

nall thing in their hopes, the foundation of which is
but contingency, but a further evill, and more finfull,
and irrationall, is, that they rejoyce in their boaftings,
they thinke by the determination of their wills to do
that which godly men doe by faith, and when their
hopes have once concluded a thing, they thinke it
fhould be eftablifhed, and thereupon runne away without reckoning with their hoaft, as wee ufe to fay,
whereas the fcripture faith, *yee ought to fay, if I live, and
if the Lord will* ; Now for their foolifh conceits to fixe
that which onely God can render certaine, is a folly
and a finne, and the hope that rifeth from it, is an irrationall prefumptuous hope, *for that they ought to fay, if
wee live, and if the Lord will*, things that are wholy out of
their power.   Now our hopes and the joy of it, *is not
a rejoycing in boafting, but it is a boafting in truth*, wee have
already the Lords will, his will declared, his will commaunded that wee fhould have the *joy of hope*, and fhould
rejoyce in hope, Rom. 12.12.   And that wee fhould have
the rejoycing of the hope firme unto the end, Heb. 3.6. So as
here is no rejoycing in boaftings, heere is no vaine
fancies of our owne, no caftles in the aire.

   But then as their is a vanity in the uncertaintie of
their hopes, which mixeth them with feares, and a further and fuller vanity, in fixeing and affureing their
hopes, by their owne boaftings and prefumptions,
incerta, certa redendo. So

3.   Thirdly, there is a mighty vanity in the matter of
their hopes, for they are of things low and meane, no
better for kinde then what they have already, why doe
they not enjoy them? nay, why doe they defpife them?
becaufe they knowe them ; fo as they defpife what
they know, and hope in what they know not, becaufe
they know it not ; but the object of our hopes, and of
                                                        our

our joy arifing from them, are of things fo great and reall, as the little, but yet the true tafte wee have of them, makes us defire more; It is our knowledge that makes us vallewe our hopes, and joy in them, and it is our ignorance that caufeth us to hope no more, nor rejoyce in the good things, which are the objects of them; And therefore wee fee faith which gives a reall evidence and fight of things, intends above any other thing our hopes, and want of faith, and weakneffe of faith leffens our hopes, and the joy of them.

The object of our hopes are things great, thing heavenly, things eternall, and thefe are the matter, if any other thing bee, of joy; Oppofite to which are the dead, beggarly, and fenfible things of this world, which are miftaken always in hope, and ufually defpifed in poffeffion, fo that not onely fimply, but in comparifon with other things, wee have all reafon for the joy of hope: The warrant of this joy wee have given you already, when wee fhewed the reafon of our joy in oppofition to wicked mens boaftings, but the end is not onely for it felf (though that be much, that wee may live comfortably, that wee be in as good a condition as this ftate is capable of) but joy as a refult and concomitant of hope, is mighty for Battaile; ye are now in the lifts, and ye put on armour, *the joy of Hope,* which is *the joy of the Lord, is our ftrength*: Hee that rejoyceth not in the hope of things to come, will rejoyce in vaine hopes, or in fenfuall enjoyments: Hee that cannot take in the pleafures of falvation by hope, will affuredly joy the joyes of wicked men, for hee wants this armour againft pleafures and fenfuall joyes, which is a weapon Sathan weilds to our dis-advantage, afmuch as any, and therefore, know how to arme your head by hope, and againft the pleafures and joyes of

X 2   this

this world, by the pleaſure and joy of hope, unleſſe you would be expoſed as a prey to things of ſence, and things of this life, againſt which this hope of ſalvation is your armour.

Object.   But now to anſwere ſhortly an objection, if hope brings in ſo great and ſteddy a returne of joy, what place will you allot for ſorrow for ſin, for wee are ſinners, and a ſinfull condition, and that affection ſuites us very well. Anſw. Certainely *wee ſhould not ſorrow*

Anſw.   *as thoſe without hope*, but as thoſe which are full of hope, yet on the other ſide, as there is occaſion, by renued acts of ſinnes, our hope and our joy ſhould intend our ſorrow, and rectify it, God would not have an uncomfortable, or a diſpairing thought, in all ſorrow, it is *the ſorrow of the world that workes death*, that deſtroyes, and hurts, ſome inordinacie, ſome exceſſe, but ſorrow intended, and relieved alſo by hope, and the joy of it, as it is often neceſſarie, ſo it will never hurt you.

1.   There is a double uſe of ſorrow, firſt to worke out the ſtaine of ſin, in ſupplying the want of afflictions: ſin is not onely evill for its tranſcient act, but for the curſed diſpoſition that it leaves behinde, there is ever ſin in the wombe of ſin, ſorrow ſerves to worke out the ſtaine of ſin, and doe the worke of afflictions, which are to humble and bring low, Prov. 20. 30. *The blewnes of a wound cleanſeth away evill, ſo doe ſtripes the inward parts of the belly*, this is applied to correction and cleanſing, afflictions worke the wound to ſuch a diſpoſition, as is cleaſing and healeing.

2.   But then ſecondly, ſorrow for ſin ſerves whereby to expreſſe our affections to Chriſt in a manner ſutable to our condition, and to the poſture wee ſtand in towards him, ſhall wee grieve the Lord, and ſhall the Lord be grieved, and ſhall wee not grieve? But hee

loves

loves us, and pardons us, therefore fhould wee grieve. Befides, while hee loves us, hee grieves, and hee grieves the more, becaufe hee loves us, and fo fhould wee, if hee did not love us, hee would not grieve, and if wee love him, wee cannot but grieve when wee offend him, Jer. 31.19. *Surely after I was turned, I repented, and after that I was inftructed, I fmote upon my thigh, I was afhamed,* &c. Ephraim mournes and grieves, which hee did not till God had mercy on him, then hee fmote on his thigh.

If you aske how wee fhould grieve? Never without the reliefe of hope, and joy, let them act and intend your forrow, but for the degree why fhould wee not in humbling our felves for fin worke our felves, and our forrow, as low as afflictions would lay us, if chaftifements fhould take hold on us, or ficknes to death, or any other hand of God chaftifing for finne, this will be no interruption in your hope, no prejudice to the joy of it.

Thus your hope armes you againft pleafures by joy, the joy of hope; but wee have paines alfo to conflict withall, all the evills and calamities, that difhonour, want, and poverty, or bodily evills can inflict, patiency alfo in attendancy and expectation, *yee have need of patience, that after yee have done the will of God, yee may receive the promife.* Wee would faine have our rewards in hand, wee are loath to ftay, wee would have the reality of the reward, not the vifion of faith onely, Heb. 10. 36. Now this is needfull, for the Saints *through faith and patience inherited the promifes,* Heb. 6. 12. If you aske who infefts the Saints, who puts them to their patience? The world and wicked men, but efpecially the Divell, that hee might difcourage us, and devoure us, might breake and interrupt our courfe, might make

X 3 us for

us for want of continuauce, doe and suffer so many
things in vaine, and therefore armes all his instruments, evill men and our owne corruptions against us,
to make us weary of that way, which is so sowed with
thornes, which costs us so much paines and trouble;
God also puts us to our patience, by suffering manifold
evills, outward and inward, to infest us, that hee might
purge present evill, and prevent further evill, and that
hee might try us, and use what hee hath laid into us,
that hee might say of us another day as hee did of *Iob*,
yee have heard of the patience of Iob, Jam. 5.11. and might
boast of us as of those induring Saints, *Heere is the
patience of the Saints*, behold it, Reu. 13.10. In all these
respects ye have need of patience, yea, and that *patience should have its perfect work*, as James saith Jam. 1.4.
That it should *possesse our soules*, that it should be fitted
for every condition, and hold out to the utmost, to
the extremitie, as you see those, who are betrusted
with forts, and strengths they had need of patience:
And yet must hold out to the utmost extremity, by
the law of warre, now then you see the need wee have
of patience, but it must be *the patience of hope*, 1. Thess.
1.3. The Apostle gives there the effects and their cau-
ses, the *work of faith*, saids hee, *the labour of love, and the
patience of hope*, the effect or great product of hope is
patience, patience is a grace which hath no shine or
glitter with it, it is sweet but darke, and obscure, and
hath nothing in it of violence, and having mighty
enemies, it defends it self in suffering, wee gaine the
victory often in loosing our lives, it scarce complaines
of what it indures, so as it passeth often amongst ignorant men for stupidity, and dulnesse. Now this sweet
and low grace (in respect of its condition, and the
manner of its operation) would be opprest a thousand
                                                    times

times under the victory of its enemies , if it were not animated by the livelinesse and activity of hope , *if the hope of salvation, the hope of glory*, ('for so it is called,) did not continually set before its eyes , the greatnesse of the reward ; yee can never have a better instance, then of our Master Christ himself while hee was in the conflict of patience, (and that was his life)hee was ever in the lists of sufferings, conflicting with sorrowes, and woes , *for the joy that was set before him* , which was made sure to him by faith, & received and enjoyed by hope, (for hee came by his comforts even as wee) this made him to *endure the crosse and despise the shame* , and wee are commanded to *runne with patience the race, that is set before us, looking to him*, Heb.12.2,3. That is, use our patience as hee did , and relieve our patience as hee did , by the joyfull sights of hope, patience without hope is the deadest thing in the world ; for why doe I deprive my self of good ? why doe I suffer so many things in vaine , if they be in vaine , and therefore the Apostle takes it for granted , that *the patient continuance in well doeing*, hath some thing to relieve it, namely , *a lookeing after glory , and honour and immortality*, &c. Rom. 2. 7. without which animation, and enlivening of hope , patience were dead , and deadly , more fit to be the property of a stone, or a blocke, then the grace of a Saint; thus yee see your selves armed by hope , against the great enemies of God and man, against the great troublers of Israel, pleasures , and paines , by having your joyes, and your patience , acted by *hope*, which is *your Helmet*.

But hope thirdly is proper for doing , aswell as suffering , having a great influence (as I told you) upon our simbolicall head, our intentions, and scopes and end, and this peece, aswell as our shooes, (*the shooes of the*

of the preparation of the Gospell of peace) inables us for
acting, and the truth is, while wee doe nothing good,
wee are not secure against doing ill ; But if hope serve
to any thing, it serves to incourage to labour, and
worke, wee use to say in a proverbe, take away hope,
and take away endeavour, no worke is done or can be
done without hope, *hee that ploweth should plow in hope,
and that hee that thresheth in hope, should be partaker of his
hopes*, 1.Cor.9.10. A man would be loath to plow the
ground, or thresh the corne without hope, you will not
doe actions of the lowest forme without it : Againe as
you can do nothing without hope, so ye attempt the
greatest things by hope, the hopes of victory, the
hope of successe, the hope of gaine, whither doth it
not ingage men, our strength depends upon our hope,
and therefore Jeremy complaines, *my strength and my
hope is perished*, Lam.3.18. No more hope, no more
strength, they stand and fall together, they are alike
in their birth and death: On the other side, when Paul
was to give an account to Agrippa of his actions,
Acts 26.6,7. *I am judged* (sayes hee) *for the hope of the promise made unto our fathers, unto which promise our twelve
tribes instantly serving God day and night hope to come.*
Doe you wonder why they served God, with that instance, and intensenesse, *day and night*, why they doe
that which none of the world doe besides, they hope
to attaine the promise of God, that is, the thing promised, that ingageth them to a continuall and a most
intense labour ; so the Apostle when hee gives in a
very few words all that is to be forborne and done for
God, and our good, makes hope to be the rise of all his
courage and activity, Tit.2.13. *lookeing for that blessed
hope, and the glorious appearing of the great God and our saviour Iesus Christ*, compared with the former verses 11.
                                                    and

and 12. *For the grace of God that bringeth salvation, hath appeared unto all men, teaching us, that denying ungodlinesse, and worldly lusts, wee should live soberly, righteously and Godly in this present world.* And Christ when hee bidds us doe any thing *hoping for nothing againe,* Luk. 6. 35. *Lend hoping for nothing againe;* hee doth not meane wee should have nothing, or be without hope, but tells us immediately, *that our reward shall be great in heaven, and wee shall be the children of the Highest,* and presently suggests matter of hope, which hee affixeth to the lending of a penny, or the giving a cup of cold water, *yee shall not loose your reward.*

But to what workes doth hope animate us ? to all for the least shall be considered, *shall not loose its reward,* and the greatest shall be considered proportionably, *Hee that overcometh, and hee that followes mee heere, shall sit upon twelve Thrones.* There is nothing so great, that hope cannot expect, for it is *the hope of salvation;* And therefore there is no worke so great, that hope cannot put you upon, for it workes from hope to salvation. Captaines when they harrang their Souldiers, tell them of the butin of the prey, tell them of honours, and advancements; and Christ when hee incourageth his, speakes Crownes as freely as any, but spirituall crownes assured by faith; and enjoyed for the present by hope; it is a shame that our hopes should not carry us toward working, as farre as ever any worldly hath done, in all the particulars of worke. I will insist onely upon one, which the scripture particularly annexeth to hope, and is proper for us all; *Hee that hath this hope,* (that is, *of seeing God, of salvation*) *hee purifyeth himself even as hee is pure,* 1. Joh. 3. 3. The reason of the action about which our hope is conversant, and the proportion lies thus, *Wee hope,* saith hee, ver. 2. *when hee shall*

Y   *appeare*

appeare to be like him, *for wee shall see him as hee is*, sayes hee there will be the same reason of your being like to him, heere and hereafter, and therefore if you will be like him in heaven, you must be like him heere, and your hope for the one, must helpe you to the other: now as in heaven hee is glorious, so heere hee was pure, ye are in all estates and conditions to follow and imitate your saviour, for that is your hope to that you were predestinated; Now hee was *holy, harmelesse, unde-filed*, therefore ye must be like in this state also.

2.　　Secondly your hope fixeth upon seeing him in hea-ven. *There shall no uncleane thing enter into the kingdome of heaven*, and therefore you must purge and cleanse your selves by the way, and your hope must do it.

This purification respecteth both the body, and the minde, and is opposed to all bodily lusts, which lies in the sences, fancie, or sensible things, and to all spiri-tuall lusts, which lie in the understanding, which lusteth against spirituall truths, and the wayes of God, sayes hee, this hope must purifie you from all this.

But how high? how farre must this hope act you, to what degrees? *Even as hee is pure*, there is your patterne, there is your examplar, study what Christ was, and be ye likewise, study what Christ did, or would doe, and doe the same; for instance, wee are apt to be proud and vaine to be supercilious, to overlooke men, and little things, to be every one for himself, gripeing and graspeing. *Purify your selves in this*, even *as hee is pure*, *let the same minde be in you that was in Christ Iesus*, Phil. 2. 5. *who though hee were in the forme of God*, debased himself, in a word consider the disposition of Christ, and consider the purity of Christ, and make that your coppy, and as you would set no bounds to glory, *you would see him as he is, and be like him*, so set no bounds to

purity.

purity, *purify your selves* after that patterne, *even as hee is pure*, and let hope and the reafon of hope doe it, becaufe you have no greater pretenfions to glory, then you have to purity, namely to be like Chrift your head, to whom by faith, and hope you are conformed. Thus yee fee your Helmet, in its glory, fecuring you from all the evill of all the goods of the world, and fecuring from all the evill of all the evill of the world, and enabling and infpiring you to work, and fervice even to all, *That you might be perfect and throughly furnifhed to every good worke*; improove therefore this bleffed peece, this hope, and get it more abundantly.

You fee it is a great matter how wee fettle our *Coroll.* hopes, becaufe in it lies the ftrength of our indeavours, wee anchor in things by hope, and fixe in them, and being fetled upon an immovable thing, wee can moove fteddily and ftronglie. Archimedes could moove the world, if hee could faften his engine, now wee caft anchor in heaven, and heavenly things in falvation, for fo fayes the Apoftle, *Wee have an anchor of the foule both fure and ftedfaft, and which entreth in to that which is within the vaile*, Heb.6.19. Our anchor cafts deepe in heaven, where there is good earthing, whence it will be, impoffible to be remooved by any ftormes or windes: But this wee muft know, that if you would make ufe of this or any armour which is fpirituall, it muft be firft raifed to a pitch, the armes muft be fafhioned, and formed, and then muft be kept bright, and in pofture, for fervice, it muft be weilded by a fpirituall hand.

Now to raife this grace, you muft improove and raife your faith, for as in all compofitions, you have fomething that gives the body of it, fo faith gives the body, and fubftance to hope, therefore faith is called the fubftance of *things hoped for*, and therefore of all

other

other things your hope will never outbid or goe beyond your faith, keep therefore that full and high.

Yet Hope is a further grace and armour, faith gives
you things in their coulours with your interefts in
them, it fhewes you that they are, and that they are
yours, but however faith gives them a kinde of prefence by beleeving, yet they are in themfelves future,
as to us, hope therefore takes in the pleafure of them
beforehand, lives in the joyfull expectation of them,
and fo abridges the time, which els would be tedious,
fancies to it felf (as I may fo fay) the pleafures and
joyes of eternall life, and lives in a fweet anticipation
of what it poffeffeth but by faith, which as it is moft
pleafant in it felf, fo it produceth mighty effects, for
joy, for patience, for working, fo as our life is comfortably entertained by it in joy, and pleafure, evills
and calamities are maftered, and fubdued by it, even
the greateft, and action and worke, the end of living
is promoted.

Therefore looke upon this peece, which hath influence into fo great effects, as a reall, not as a notionall
thing, as a thing that many want in the ufe and exer-
cife of it, but they cannot live without it, they cannot
live a vitall life animated with joy, armed with patience
and acted, to worke and fervice.

Therefore let not fo great an engine of the Holy
Ghoft, fo great and good an armour lye dead by us, but
rather let us improove it, and ufe it, try alwayes of
raifing it, for it is raifed and improoved grace that
workes great and confiderable effects.

--- *And the fword of the fpirit which is the word of God.*
This is the laft peece of armes, and is fitted both for
offence, and defence, it is an armes that is great alone,
and therefore men arme themfelves with this, which
ufe

ufe no other, and it is alfo an appendix to all armes,
for no man is armed at all points, like a fouldier, which
hath not a fword, this is a peece of a very expedite,
and continuall ufe.

You need not goe farre to know what this fword is,
the Apoftle defcribes it firft by being the fword of the
fpirit, that is, a fpirituall fword, *The weapons of our war-*
fare are not carnall, but mighty through God, 2.Cor. 10. 4.
The Divell will not give way or yeild to a fword made
of any other mettall, therefore it is *mighty through God :*
The Egyptians are flesh, and not fpirit, therefore they are
weake. One Divell is able to deale with all the flefhly
and carnall weapons in the world, it is not charmes,
and holy water, nor refolutions, and purpofes, and
reafonings alone, that are weapons fit for this combate, they muft be things truely fpirituall.

But then fecondly, it is that fword, which the fpirit
ufeth in us, and by us, the fpirit of God, the Holy
Ghoft, fo as there is a mighty arme, to a mighty
weapon, *For wee know not how to pray as wee ought,* how to
doe any thing, *but the fpirit maketh interceffion in us*, and
it is *the fpirit that leads us into all truth*, and teacheth us
how to ufe, and improove truth, without the fpirit of
God, the word of God woulddoe us no good ; The
weapon would be too heavy, to unweildy for us to ufe,
therefore faith the Apoftle, *The weapons of our warfare*
are mighty through God, 2.Cor.10.4. God muft ufe, and
guide the hand, afwell as give the fword, it will be els
like the weapons of a mighty man in the hand of a
childe, if hee take it up, it will be but to let it fall.

But then thirdly, *it is the fword of the fpirit*, the fpirit   3.
doth not onely ufe it, but hee formed it, it is therefore
fit for ufe, becaufe hee formed it, that is the mighty
worke-man, and Engineer for fpirituall weapons, and

hee

hee muſt be able to uſe it well , that made it , for hee
made it for uſe, and there is no ingredient in it, which
hath not an influence into the end of it , which is the
uſe of it.   Now that hee formed, it appeares 2.Pet.1.
20,21. *Prophecy came not in old time (or at any time) by the*
will of man , that is , by the preſumptuous will of bold
men, proudly , and arrogantly goeing about to determine,that by their will,which by their reaſons and un-
ſtandings could not reach , *but holy men of God ſpake , as*
they were mooved by the Holy Ghoſt ; God uſed the under-
derſtandings and the wills of holy men , to derive and
conveye his truth to the world , ſo 2.Tim.3.16. *All*
ſcripture is given by inſpiration of God , ſo as the ſpirit
formes it,frames it, ſuggeſts it,brings it to the world.

Thus having knowne the matter of this ſword, that
it is ſpirituall, not of a carnall make , or compoſition,
and ſecondly the mannager and weilder of this ſword,
that it is the ſpirit, and then the maker, and former of
this ſword, that it is the ſame ſpirit, wee come now to
the appellation it ſelf , which the ſpirit gives it, which
is *the word of God.*

1.   By the word of God is meant , what ever God hath
made knowne to be his will , as it is contained in the
ſcripture.

This muſt needs bee the word of God,and no other,
but as it is conſonant to this , for in a large ſenſe , all
truths may be called the word of God, as being ſubjected to ſome ſcripture rule , but ſtrictly that word
which is our ſword, is ſome portion of that wee call
the ſcripture, which is particularly characterized,and
diſtinguiſhed by this title *the word of God.*

This muſt needs be ſo , becauſe this is that , which
muſt not be added to,or detracted from , it muſt ſtand
alone Deut.4.2. *Yee ſhall not adde unto the word , which*
                                                  I com-

I command you, neither shall you diminish ought from it : Therefore that is all, and onely the word of God : So Deut.12.32. Gal.1.8. *If wee or Angell from heaven preach any other Gospell unto you, then that which wee have preached to you, let him be accursed.*

Secondly, if God will have the ballance of the Sanctuary for waights, and measures, for rules and determinations, it must be visible, and publique : If hee will have us fight with such weapons, wee must know where to fetch them.

Thirdly, when wee see this rule in practise by Christ or his Apostles, wee see this word taken up for this sword, to doe mighty things.

Wee see Christ resisting the Divell, and at last confounding and expelling him by this word, by this weapon, Math.'4.4. Hee followed him so long with *It is written,* that at last hee drove him quite away, hee resisted him by this sword, till hee fled from him.

As hee dealt with the Divell in himself, so he dealt with the Divell in the Scribes and Pharises, *Have yee not read* (saith he) *what David did, and what the Priests did, &c.* Math. 12.3,4,5. So hee answered them, and confounded them ; The like did Stephen, and the Apostles, *convinced men mightily by the Scriptures, that Iesus was the Christ,* and used this sword to destroy unbeliefe with. Now this word of God, which is our sword, is not so much the letter of the word, as the sense of it, how unreasonably and foolishly have the Papists abused themselves by sticking to the letter, in those words, *This is my body,* and Origen in making himself an Eunuch, from that place, Math.19.12. *There be Eunuchs that have made themselves Eunuchs for the Kingdome of heavens sake.* Though it be also true that where the letter is not contrary to the Annalogy of faith, that is to be our rule and guide, and upon no other ground are wee to depart from the letter.

But if it be objected, how shall men especially unlearned, know the sence of Scripture, which seemes sometimes to be subject to contrariety? *Answ.* This is the great grace of God towards his, that in things necessary to faith and manners, to be knowne, or done, they need not be ignorant, for *they walke in the light of the Lord*, by virtue of which light they are led into *all truth*; so as they need not pin, their faith upon the authority of anothers judgment; This is there due by promise, *They shall be all taught of God*, Isa. 54. 13. and Christ sayes, *his sheepe follow him, because they know his voice, but another they will not follow, because they know not the voice of strangers*, Joh. 10. 4, 5. To have the word made cleare to you, and this sword fit for your use, is your due aswell as the sword it self. So *the secret of the Lord is with them that feare him*, Psal. 25. 14. The scriptures though deepe are foordable by those who are holy, and diligent, though they be not so wise and learned: On the other side, *The naturall man knoweth not the things that are of the spirit of God, because they are foolishnesse to him: But the spirituall man knoweth all things*, 1. Cor. 2. 14, 15. So

1. John 5. 6: *It is the spirit that beareth witnesse, because the spirit is truth.* And ver. 10. *Hee that beleeveth on the Son of God, hath the witnesse in himselfe.* So Math. 13. 11. *To you it is given to know the misteries of the Kingdome of heaven, to others it is not given.* There is a sence of Scripture that lyes alwayes not so evident and above, but it is given to you as your peculiar, and portion.

This honour have all the Saints, they have a certaine taste sutable and proportionable to their spirits, and their new natures, by which they can distinguish of food,

and

and by which they can try all things, for as to other
lives, and to our bodily, there is a taſt for that end, ſo
to this alſo which is ſpirituall ; And though men in a
dreame can not diſtinguiſh betweene ſleeping, and waking, yet men that are awake , know they are awake,
and know alſo diſtinctly what they doe.

This notwithſtanding, God ſells all thing to us by
labour, and wee ſhall not enjoy the benefit of this
great priviledge without it; Wee muſt therefore keepe
our ſelves in a holy frame : *If any man will doe his will, he
ſhall know of his Doctrine whether it be of God*, Joh. 7. 17.
While wee are doeing , wee are in a way to know. If
you be *carnall and walke as men, you will be alſo carnall, and
judge as men*, Rom. 8. 8. *They that are in the fleſh cannot
pleaſe God* , (which may be underſtood alſo of a fleſhly
frame in the Saints) and when wee are in a way altogether unpleaſing to God, God will not accommodate
himſelf, will not reveale himſelf to us, and pleaſe us.

But this is not enough, *wee muſt ſearch the ſcriptures, in
which wee thinke to have eternall life*, and light alſo for the
way thither , wee muſt conſider , and weigh whether
thoſe things which our owne reaſon, or the Miniſtry
of others repreſent to us, be ſo or no, as thoſe of Bærea
did, *Truth lies deepe, errors lyeth levell to all* : This ſearch
is extreamely pleaſing to God , ſince the ſubject of it
is the knowledge of his will , and the end of it is the
doing of his will ; This is done by much meditation
in the word, by comparing, by examining it, by taking
in all aydes , and helpes of the guiſts and abilities of
others , for God hath ordered that one man ſhould
need another, that none might be perfect alone ; nothing alſo will more advance it then prayer, ſo Paul
prayed often *for the ſpirit of revelation*, and David *that his
eyes might be enlightened* , to ſee the wonderfull things of Gods

Z   law ;

law; nothing cleares the eye-fight more then prayer, for that sets your ends right, and makes you fit for light, and that leads you into the presence of God, into his light, *in n hose light wee see light.*

It was necessary to speake some thing of this, because this is the forming and shaping of your weapon, the weapon may be shaped in it self, but not to us; this gives the mettall to the sword, if a thing looke like the word of God and be not, that will not cut of your lusts, it will proove but a leaden sword, or a deceitfull bow, that will not reach the marke, it will be *a carnall weapon*, which is weake, whereas the other is *mighty through God.*

Coroll.   To incourage you against spirituall enemies, because ye have spirituall armes, and spirituall weapons ye have, what to keep of blowes, and yee have wherewith to fight and combate with your adversaries : God hath not left us fatherlesse, nor hee hath not left us weaponlesse, hee deales not as Pharoah, commands us to make bricks, and takes away materialls, hee doth not disarme us, and bid us fight, but hee gives us armes proper for the field of combate, and for the enemy wee dispute with, and hee stands by, and lookes on, and with voyce, and hand incourageth us, so as wee need not feare our enemies, hee gives us the best armes : Good commanders, and officers, the holy Spirit, and holds a crowne over our heads: The truth is, wee never are overcome, but when wee are of the party, when wee are in a proportion false to God, and our enemy hath gained us, then wee fight but for a shew, and the weapon falls easily out of our hands, but if wee would stand to it, our sword would cut his cords, and if hee did stand two or three thrusts, hee would vanish at last, as hee did from Christ our captaine.

That

That wee may the better ufe this fword, wee fhall do well. Firft to vallew it, things that wee prize and vallew, wee willingly ufe, wee thinke they will effect their end, els wee lay them by. Therefore wee fhall pitch upon fome expreffions, that may teach us to vallew this weapon, when Abiathar had mentioned the fword of Goliah, there is none like that, faith David, the dignities of the word are great, as appeares by David efpecially, who meditated in the law continually, and as much as any vallewed the word.

Pfal.17.4. *Concerning the workes of mens hands, by the word of thy lips, I have kept mee from the path of the deftroyer,* the word that God fpake was that, which armed him againft wicked men.

Pfal.18.30. *The word of the Lord is tryed* (or refined) *hee is a Buckler to all that truft him; As for God his way is perfect,* it is a fure word, and which hath bene often experienced, tryed againe and againe, fo as you may venture upon it, as upon a thing that will not faile, or deceive, will not ftart afide, *like a deceitfull and broken bow.*

Pfal.119.11. *Thy word have I hid in my heart, that I might not fin againft thee;* David knew the ufe of this, that it would preferve him from fin, and therefore ftored it up, hid it in a fure place, againft a time of need.

Ver.89. *For ever O Lord, thy word is fetled in heaven;* It is an unchangeable rule, which will never alter, and fetled, will attaine all it pretends to.

Ver.105. *Thy word is a lampe to my feete, and a light unto my pathes;* this is againft delufions, and faynts, and fhaddowes, the Divell will caft. If you keep neere the word, you carry a light in your hand, you will not fight in the darke, but know how to make your addreffes, and approaches, and how to order your wards, and defenfes.

Ver.140. *Thy word is very pure, therefore thy servant loveth it* ; every thing operates as it is, as things are to their beings, so they are to their operations. That which is pure will render us pure, and the word is not an idle thing, but for use, and being pure, it is given us to render us pure.

Ver. 172. *My tongue shall speake of thy word, for all thy commandements are righteous* ; I can never praise them enough, there is such a law of righteousnes in them.

Psal. 147. 19. *Hee sheweth his word unto Iacob, his statutes and his judgements unto Israel;* from the receivers of the dispensation of the word, you see its excellency, it is the portion onely of his people, it is not flung in common to the world, as an inconsiderable thing.

Isa. 40. 8. *The grasse withereth, and the flower fadeth, but the word of the Lord shall stand for ever* ; the excellency of good things lies in the continuance of them, this hath a good warrant for its abiding, because it is the word of the abiding, and unchangeable God.

Isa. 55. 10, 11. *For as the raine cometh downe and the snow from heaven, and returneth not thither, but watereth the earth, and maketh it bring forth and bud, that it may give seed to the sower, and bread to the eater : so shall my word be that goeth forth out of my mouth, it shall not returne unto me voyd, but it shall accomplish that which I please, and it shall prosper in the thing where to I sent it.* There is a mighty efficacy in this word, this lies as a praise upon the whole word of God, that it shall not returne empty, but be *like the bow of Ionathan, and the sword of Saul,* Isay. 66. 2. *All those things hath my hand made, but to this man will I looke even to him that is poore and of a contrite spirit, and trembleth at my word.* That word is precious, when the respect to it is so rewarded. On the other side.

Jer.

Jer. 8. 9. *They have rejected the word of the Lord, and what wisedome is in them.* Though otherwise they might be wise, yet if they undervallew once the word, they bid a dewe to their wisedome : And God the righteous judge, and which gives true vallewes to us, rankes them in the number of fooles, from the New Testament also, wee shall give some places to this purpose.

Luk. 4. 4. *Men lives by every word of God;* in him wee live, and in his word wee live, which gives a being to things that which gives the being, and determination, makes things be what they are, and men doe what they doe, must needs be great and excellent in it self.

Ver. 32. *His word was with power,* which astonied the auditours.

Ver. 36. *What a word is this, for with authority and power commandeth hee the uncleane spirits, and they come forth;* his word will fetch uncleannes out of thy heart, aswell as out of their bodies.

Luk. 7. 7. The centurion had so much confidence in Chrifts word, as hee could depend wholy upon it, *Say in a word,* (sayes hee) *and my servant shall be healed;* the magnifing of the word, wrought this great effect, and that word must needs be great, which was deservedly the object of such a confidence.

Luk. 22. 61. *Peter remembred the words of the Lord, and hee went out and wept bitterly :* Peter forgot the word, when hee sinned, and indeed all sin proceeds from ignorance or forgetfulnesse, but when hee remembred it, you see the eminent effect of it, hee repents immediately, which hee witnesseth by his bitter and abundant weeping.

John 15. 3. *Now are ye cleane through the word which I have spoken to you :* Wee are cleane mistically by the washing of Baptisme, 1. Cor. 6. 11. also by the imputa-

tion

tion of Chrifts purity, and fo wee ftand ever cleare before God, wee are pure alfo in the change of our owne
hearts, and all this by the word, made ours by faith, and
abiding in us, fo *that as evill communication corrupts good
manners* ; if taken in and drunke downe, fo the word
taken downe cleanfeth, Acts 13.26. *It is called the word
of falvation*, that which brings it and workes it. And

Acts 20.32. When Paul departed from Ephefus, *hee
commended the Church to the word of Gods grace, which was
able to build them up, and to give them an inheritance, &c.*
The inheritance is that to which the word leads us,
and where it will leave us at the laft, but before you
come thither, there is building work, forming and
fafhioning, that the word doth alfo, fo as yee need not
goe out of this circle, for the beginning or finifhing of
your faith.

2. Cor. 5.18. *It is the word of reconciliation*, that which
brings God and man together : Wee are naturally at
great diftances, now that which conduceth to the
meeting, and according of termes fo differing, muft
needs be of great vallew and efteeme.

1. Tim. 4. 5. *For every creature of God is good and nothing
to be refufed, if it be received with thanksgiving, for it is fancti-
fied by the word of God and prayer;* it is the word of God
that fanctifieth, and gives a lawfull ufe of all things;
Hence you have your liberties, afwell to indifferent,
as your right to things neceffary, if you have whereof
freely to ufe for your owne comforts, and whereof to
give away, for the weakneffe and fcandall of your
brother.

If you fhould examine by experience the effects of
the word, Gods word hath ever taken hold of men, and
in this lies the great difference of the Saints from
others, that they obferve thofe events, which others
neglect,

neglect, and growe by them. Joh. 4. 50. *And the man beleeved the word of God, and it was even so as hee had beleeved;* The word hath ever found out men, and will take hold of us, either by our faith for good, or without it for our destruction, so the prophecies of old were not idle, but effected the end for which they came.

To conclude this great dignity the word hath, that it gives its owne credit, for reason may be opposed by reason, but this is higher then reason : The Divell can reason and distinguish us into sin, whilst wee fight at that weapon, but bring him a word, and that answeres his reason.

What hath bene said in this head, tends to begit in you a right vallew and esteeme of the word, which if once ye have you will use it, and have recourse to it at all times, as an effectuall weapon, *mighty through God,* for all the great ends you have heard of.

Secondly, know the word of God, that yee may use it, this is to have your weapon prepared, you must search the fence, know the Annalogie of faith and the proportion, one truth holds to another, as before. | 2.

Thirdly, take up this sword, take it to you, be in a posture to give a blow, or to evade one, wound the enemy when you can, and meete with his blowes and thrusts, therefore you must be prepared, and have things in readinesse, therefore *the word of God* must *dwell richly in you,* that you may not be to seeke when you should use it. | 3.

To helpe you in some guards for this fight.

First, that sin is the greatest evill, mannage your sword well for that guard, have words at hand, that is, your sword ready to make that good; for the filthinesse of it, sin is compared to the blood and pollution of a new borne child, before it be ordered and dressed,

Ezek.

Ezek. 16.6. *When thou waſt in thy blood, I ſaid unto thee live*; ſuch a thing is ſin in it ſelf, and all ſin holds of the nature of that pollution.

1. *Joh.* 5. 19. *The whole world lieth in wickedneſſe*, it lies there as in a filthy grave, rotting and ſtinking as in a puddle.

Againe ſin is compared for its nature to ſwine, and dogs, and to their vomit, 2. *Pet.* 2. 22. the ſinner is the dogg in the act of ſin, and the corruption is the vomit, and mire; it is likened alſo to the menſtruouſneſſe of a woman, to a veſſell *in which is no pleaſure*, that is, a draught or a privy, *Hoſ.* 8. 8. If beſides theſe abaſings and vilifying expreſſions, you would know more of ſin: It was ſinne that condemned the world in Adam, drowned the world in the dayes of Noah, and to give you a greater charracter for ill then all this, it was ſin brought all the ſufferings upon Chriſt which hee endured: It was *the day of Gods fierce anger*, Lament. 1. 12. *When Chriſt did beare the ſins of many in his body on the tree*; therefore when Paul and Silas could ſing in the priſon, and the Saints in their afflictions, as they have done ſo often, Chriſt was low, and poore, and faint. Why? becauſe hee conflicted with ſinne, hee grappled with ſinne, *upon him was laid the iniquities of us all*; Hee conflicted with the wrath of God, for ſinne, and had hee not bene God himſelf, hee would never have outwraſtled it.

In a word every creature of God is good, and nothing offends him, irritates him, and provokes him, but ſinne; Nothing reacheth God, nor cauſeth God to reach the world in anger but ſinne. It is that which puts the ſting into death, and torment in Hell; Thus you are armed for that guard, that ſin is the greateſt evill, the ſecond followes eaſily. That then.

Wee

Wee should keep at the greatest distance from it, for that you have Rom. 12.9. *Abhorre that which is evill, cleave to that which is good*, when wee meete with any thing extreamely evill, and contrary to us, nature abhorres it, and retyres as farre as it can; so on the contrary *cleave to that which is good*, cling to it, as a man should cleave to his wife, or be glewed, as the word is, *and they shall be one flesh*, incorporate your selves with that which is good, make your self one with it.

So, *Abstaine from all appearance of evill*, 1. Thess. 5.22. a thing may appeare to be ill, that is not, but take heed of any similitude, or appearance, or likenesse of ill, if it looke like ill, though it bee not, fly from it; This gives you the benefit of a long sword, by which you keep the enemy at a distance; so Jude 23. *Hate the garments spotted with the flesh*, not onely the flesh, but the garment that hath toucht it.

Ephes. 5.3. *Fornication and all uncleannes and covetousnesse, let it not be once named among you, as becometh Saintes, nor filthinesse, nor foolish speaking, nor jesting.*

So Job 31.1. *I made a covenant with mine eyes, why should I thinke on a maide*; hee would not looke, because hee would not thinke, and the way to secure the thoughts, is to keepe well and strictly, the out-doores, the fences, which made David pray to God, to turne away his eyes from vanity. Folly is bold, but wisdome is wary to keepe at the greatest distance.

Thus this sword cuts of the first risings, this is a sure way, and this saves you a world of paines, when a temptation or a lust hath once come within you, and incorporated it self, you must teare your flesh to pull it out, you must pull up earth and all, that the roots may come at last; but while it is at a distance, there is some kinde of modesty, and blushing in it, and it may

be

be fnib'd with a word, ufe therefore fome of thefe for a fword in time, and it may prevent you hard work, which yet muft be done if you would not perifh; other heads I thought to have runne over and fitted for ufe, as

Thirdly, God knowes our thoughts.

Fourthly, that the word muft judge us even this, which wee have in our hands and mouthes, and if it condemne our finnes now, how is it like to acquit us another day.

Fifthly, that every fecret thing fhall be made manifeft.

Sixtly, that you fhould walke in the fence of death and changes, but I fhall profecute this no further, onely let us know, that if the Divell have got within us, the fame way hee is fetcht out, that hee is kept out, this fword muft do both. Thus God hath armed you compleatly, and it will be both your fin, which you will not know how to anfwer, and your fhame alfo to be foyled.

If you oppofe Captaine to Captaine, you have Chrift and the Divell, you have as fufficient, as mighty, as experienced, a Captaine as your lufts have, if armes to armes, yee have all thefe fpirituall armes, againft his carnall armes, for fo are his, in comparifon of thofe. Though his be fpirituall alfo, as acted by a mighty fpirit; your reward held over you by hope, is greater for the prefent then any he can offer, though not to flatter our felves. Our condition heere is to *indure hardneffe as good fouldiers,* 2. Tim. 2. 3. And wee muft conflict according to the law of combate, if wee would have the crowne; But this is no new thing to us, this wee knew when wee undertooke religion, this was laid in at firft, as the law and condition of our undertaking.

That

That which followes, is prayer, *praying with all prayer*, which is to all other ordinances of God as bread and falt to our repaft, wee cannot make a meale without it, heere it faftens on your armour, and lookes up for ftrength and fucceffe to him who is able to give it: If fouldiers be weake or fuccumbe in fight, they fend to their Generall for fupplies, and reinforcements.

Praying alwayes, that is in all time, & every juncture, and article of time, as you have occafion by temptations for combate, for fo καιρ☺, fignifies properly occafion, this is not fo much fpoken heere of our ordinary, and cuftomary ufe of Prayer, as it is applicable to occafions, that is temptations, but this Prayer muft be *in the fpirit :* The Spirit in our Prayer is what the foule is in our bodie, it is that which gives the life to it, to conflict with the living God by dead words, will doe no good, therefore Jude fayth, *Praying in the Holy Ghoft,* ver. 20. You have another expreffion Rom. 8. That *the fpirit makes interceffion for us,* the Holy Ghoft muft pray in us, there muft be an incorporating in that duty of the Holy Spirit, with our fpirits, *watching thereunto,* you muft watch to prayer, therefore it muft be an act of time.

With all perfeverance, that is, till the worke be done, for then ye perfevere, when ye give not over till you obtaine your end, fo as your Praying, and fighting muft runne parralell till you have overcome your enemie, and fleighted his workes.

Its enough to have hinted this which I intend not to fpeake of as being no peece of the armour, nor refembled by the Holy Ghoft to any peece.

To all that hath bene faid, I fhall adde no more but this, that every thing is ftrong in vertue of an ordinance, therefore bread nourifheth, becaufe it hath a

word

word that bids it doe fo, and therefore the word fhall cut and deftroy, becaufe God hath made it a fword, and edged and fitted it, for that purpofe.

Thus have I fome what largely meafured the field of Battaile, fhewed you your friends and enemies, and fitted to you thofe armes which God hath given you for the fervice of this holy warre.

To conclude therefore, The juft end and defigne of warre (for every thing is to act in vertue of a defigne) is peace, now no warre pretends to peace more then this we have been fpeaking of, and therefore Communion, which is the effect, and birth of peace, beares one halfe of the title of this difcourfe; And indeed men were fo form'd for Communion, as no doctrine can be avowed for good, which renders them unfociable. But experience tells us, that it is the fate of fome warres, not onely to be the meanes by which peace is gotten, and procur'd, but by which it is nourifht, and maintayn'd, and we know fome countryes, which injoy the greateft benefites of peace in the midft of a confirm'd warre. And that is efpecially the condition of the warre we have been fpeaking of, that it procures, and makes good our peace; it is the wall of our citty wherein peace dwells, it is the armes of our perfons, the fubject of it; For with the divell our profeft and avowed enemy, God hath juftly determin'd an everlafting warre. Peace, we know, is the daughter of equality, but where both partyes (as here) pretend peremptorily to fupremacy, there can be no peace. Peace alfo is the birth of love, and love is an union of mindes, but where principles are layd in by nature, or form'd by oppofition (as here) infinitly diftant, there peace can be nothing. But an abuf'd, and miftaken name of what is not, and the product of fuch a truce or peace, would

would be to procure no leſſe aſſured, but a more une-
quall warre, then what it ſeem'd to determine, as the
experience of all, who have manadg'd this warre, witneſſe: The bleſſings therefore of our peace will be
reapt within the compaſſe of our aſſured friends, and
allyes, with whom our communion will be intended &
exerciſed, as otherwiſe, ſo by a common determination
againſt the enemy: And to meete in a common enmity, where it is juſt, makes particularly, and warran-
tably to love. In a word therefore, we improve beſt
our communion with our friends, the good Angells,
whilſt we make warre, ſo as whilſt we make warre, we
ſhall have peace.

F I N I S.

Aa 3   A Table

A Table directing to severall particulars, in the præceding discours.

Foure

Severall

THE TABLE.

Do

Bb   Coroll.

The

THE TABLE.

God

FINIS.

These principall faults escaped in the printing, the Reader may correct as followeth.

Pag.	Line.	Error.	Correct.	Pag.	Line.	Error.	Correct.
2	27	with	which	108	30	all	will
9	2	incorporall	incorporeall	110	17	deferred	deterred
10	20	that	their		20	the proper	the divells proper
11	24	beingh	beings	116	24	obstaine	obtaine
13	28	them	then	117	9	hee	yee
16	28	operations	apparitions	119	18	devotes	denotes
19	16	genui	genium		21	clumbs	clumbes
23	3	*pro ratio*	*pur ratio*		22	in	is
23	27	moderatedly	moderated by	120	22	lounes	loaves
28	4	ward	word	129	29	*subsilie*	*sulfilire*
	5	sunne	sonne	133	4	temire	tenure
	9	Mathematicus,	Mathematicians	136	13	imployes	implyes
30	20	God	things	137	11	helpe is	helpes
31	14	not	*must be put out.*		26	of from	of well from
33	28	raisedned	raisednes	140	13	jou	you
34	31	medimus	mediums	141	18	but	put
38	2	beleeve	releeve	142	30	him	sinne
39	14	light	sight	143	26	counted	committed
49	23	may	by	144	10	countinent	commitment
	25	vice	nice		17	inections	injections
50	14	motion	notion	145	4	that	thus
	18	and	*must be put out.*	146	17	all	allye
	19	their	your	147	17	nothing as	nothing so much as
51	5	with	which	148	25	not	*must be put out.*
	15	Elixurs	Elixars	150	27	fin	sinne
	33	ones	ends	151	13	is	was
52	24	well	*must be put out.*		14	have	save
55	25	let	set		21	mottinesse	motives
58	22	the	they	154	21	fault	faint
61	18	mote	more	155	12	principall	principle
63	7	your	you		23	pates	pathes
	33	not	not onely		30	toward	to warde
73	5	to operating	co-operating	159	10	fasten	fasten'd
77	30	inordinary	inordinacy		29	in other	in no other
78	10	thy	the		33	allocy	allay
79	10	hee	be	160	26	ofter	after
86	9	have	save	161	5	contingenties	contingencies
89	20	altogether	together	164	8	and a	and in a
	31	*forma*	*forma*		29	cleasing	cleansing
91	22	which	what	165	23	patiency	patience
97	26	a love	alone	170	15	respecteth	respecteth
98	33	must	most	174	8	by	*must be put out.*
99	5	therefore is	therefore that is		9	unstandings	understandings
100	8	that is	that it is	182	27	if	*must be put out.*
103	24	peoples	puples				